Finding Chr
Your Ma

A Guided Discovery for Groups and Individuals

Kevin and Louise Perrotta

LOYOLAPRESS.

CHICAGO

LOYOLAPRESS.

3441 N. ASHLAND AVENUE
CHICAGO, ILLINOIS 60657
(800) 621-1008
WWW.LOYOLABOOKS.ORG

Nihil Obstat	*Imprimatur*
Reverend James P. McIlhone, Ph.D.	Reverend George J. Rassas
Censor Deputatus	Vicar General
June 18, 2005	Archdiocese of Chicago
	July 5, 2005

Unless otherwise noted, the Scripture quotations contained herein are from the New Revised Standard Version Bible: Catholic Edition, copyright © 1993 and 1989 by the Division of Christian Education of the National Council of the Churches of Christ in the U.S.A. Used by permission. All rights reserved. Subheadings in Scripture quotations have been added by Kevin and Louise Perrotta.

Excerpts from the English translation of Rite of Marriage © 1969, International Committee on English in the Liturgy, Inc. All rights reserved.

The quotations from John Paul II (p. 31) are taken from his book *The Theology of the Body* (Boston: Pauline Books & Media, 1997), 369.

The quotation from Othmar Keel (p. 37) is taken from *The Song of Songs: A Continental Commentary,* trans. Frederick J. Gaiser (Minneapolis: Fortress Press, 1994).

The quotations from John Paul II (p. 71) are taken from his book *Letter to Families from Pope John Paul II: 1994 Year of the Family* (Boston: Pauline Books & Media, 1994), 89–90.

Interior design by Kay Hartmann/Communique Design
Illustration by Anni Betts

ISBN 0-8294-2142-4

Printed in the United States of America
06 07 08 09 10 11 Bang 10 9 8 7 6 5 4 3 2 1

Contents

How to Use This Guide

If you want to explore marriage, the natural place to begin is the Bible. Because the Holy Spirit guided the authors of Scripture, the book they wrote is an always-fresh source of wisdom on everything concerning God and our relationship with him, and our most important personal relationships, such as marriage.

In this book we will read excerpts from various places in Scripture to learn about what marriage is and how to live it out successfully according to God's purposes. The goal is to grow in our understanding and appreciation for marriage—and, for those of us who are married, to grow in love for one another as spouses.

Our approach will be a *guided discovery.* It will be *guided* because we all need support in understanding Scripture and reflecting on what it means for our lives. Scripture was written to be understood and applied in the community of faith, so we read the Bible *for* ourselves but not *by* ourselves. Even if we are reading alone rather than in a group, we need resources that help us grow in understanding. Our approach is also one of *discovery,* because each of us needs to encounter Scripture for ourselves and consider its meaning for our life. No one can do this for us.

This book is designed to give you both guidance for understanding and tools for discovery.

The introduction on page 6 will guide your reading by providing background material and helping you get oriented to the subject of our exploration. Each week, a brief "Background" section will give you context for the reading, and the "Exploring the Theme" section that follows the reading will bring out the meaning of the Scripture passages. Supplementary material between sessions will offer further resources for understanding.

The main tool for discovery is the "Questions for Reflection and Discussion" section in each session. Choose the questions you think will work best for you. Preparing to answer all the questions ahead of time is highly recommended.

We suggest that spouses pay particular attention to the final question each week, labeled "Focus question." This question points to an especially important issue about marriage raised by the reading. Do leave enough time to discuss it!

Other sections encourage you to take an active approach to your Bible reading and discussion. At the start of each session, "Questions to Begin" will help you break the ice and start talk flowing. Often these questions are light and have only a slight connection to the reading. After each Scripture reading, there is a suggested time for a "First Impression." This gives you a chance to express a brief, initial, personal response to the text. Each session ends with a "Prayer to Close" that suggests a way of expressing your response to God.

How long are the discussion sessions? We've assumed you will have about an hour and twenty minutes. If you have less time, you'll find that most of the elements can be shortened somewhat.

Is homework necessary? You will get the most out of your discussions if you read the weekly material and prepare your answers to the questions in advance of each meeting. If participants are not able to prepare, read the "Exploring the Theme" sections aloud at the points where they appear.

What about leadership? You don't have to be an expert in the Bible to lead a discussion. Choose one or two people to act as discussion facilitators, and have everyone in the group read "Suggestions for Bible Discussion Groups" (page 92) before beginning.

Does everyone need a guide? a Bible? Everyone in the group will need their own copy of this book. It contains the biblical texts, so a Bible is not absolutely necessary—but each person will find it useful to have one. You should have at least one Bible on hand for your discussions. (See page 96 for recommendations.)

Before you begin, take a look at the suggestions for Bible discussion groups (page 92) or individuals (page 95).

Why do some people cry at weddings? As they look at the bride and groom holding hands up there by the altar, parents and siblings know they are suffering a loss. The older among us, suddenly feeling the slippage of time, are reminded of our age and mortality. Probably the main reason for wedding tears, however, is beauty—the beauty of the bride, and a deeper beauty. "It's wonderful that John and Katherine found each other. It's so beautiful to see them deeply in love—so beautiful that there *is* such love in the world."

But what will happen to the beauty? Katherine and John will have to deal with much that is unlovely, including some stuff they discover in each other. Will their marriage lose its glow? Some spouses become bored with each other, angry, disappointed, cynical. Their marriages degenerate into a resigned modus vivendi or an armed truce. One hears, "If I could afford it, I'd leave," and, eventually, "I'm out of here." Or, John and Katherine's marriage may be one of those where husband and wife go on holding hands through the rough stretches of life. The beauty that flashed briefly at their wedding may shine even more brightly as the years go by.

Whether the beauty grows or goes out will depend on whether Katherine and John move closer to its source. Will they find Christ in their marriage—and see their marriage and themselves more clearly in his light?

This book is designed to help every John and Katherine—those of you just starting out together and those who have made it some ways down the marital road—to ponder your marriage in the light of Christ. The book is also intended for everyone else—those of you who are unmarried, are planning not to marry, or are no longer married. Marriage is well worth exploring, whether we are inside or outside of it, whether we are looking forward to it or looking back on it.

For our exploration, we have taken our cue from Jesus. Asked about marriage, he referred the questioner to Scripture (Mark 10:6–9; Genesis 1:27; 2:24). Following his lead, we will investigate some passages in Scripture that contribute to an understanding of marriage—what it is, how to live it, how to find Christ in it. The Bible is not a detailed how-to manual for marriage, but it supplies us with a wealth of inspired insight into the marriage relationship and into the attitudes and approaches that lead to success.

The agenda for our explorations comes from the wedding liturgy. Through the vows, prayers, and blessings, the wedding liturgy expresses the Catholic understanding of marriage. Each of our six weekly sessions revolves around a prominent theme in the wedding liturgy. The Scripture passages have been chosen to unfold the themes. Since the themes are interconnected and the Scripture passages are rich in meaning, it will be helpful, before we set out, to get an idea of where we are going.

Week 1. "I, David, take you, Erin, for my lawful wife . . . I, Erin, take you, David, for my lawful husband . . . from this day forward . . . until death do us part."

In marriage, the taking is accomplished only through giving. David takes Erin only by offering himself to her. Taking rightly requires recognizing the infinite worth of the one received. Let Erin accept the gift of David with a sense of his incomparable value!

Our biblical readings speak to us about marriage as a many-sided gift. The Old Testament creation accounts remind us that life itself is God's gift—and that the design of marriage, and our being designed for it, are among God's basic gifts to us. In a New Testament passage, St. Paul tells us that Christian marriage is modeled on Christ's total gift of self. Paul presents marriage as a special opportunity to enter into Christ's self-giving.

Paul lays the groundwork for the Catholic understanding of marriage as a sacrament. A sacrament is a visible sign of God's invisible grace, an earthly reality through which Christ acts in our lives. In Baptism, for example, it is water; in Confirmation, oil. In marriage, the sign is the spouses themselves. In the wedding ceremony the ring is a sign. Erin and David each say, "Take this ring as a sign of my love and fidelity." But then *David and Erin* become the sign of God's love and fidelity—David a sign of God's generosity and faithfulness to Erin, Erin a sign of this to David. From the moment the spouses pledge their lifelong, exclusive commitment to each other, they are "the full and real visible sign of the sacrament itself," Pope John Paul II writes. As a couple, they will become a sign of God's love to others, especially to their children.

Week 2. "I, Stephen, take you, Audra, for my lawful wife . . . I, Audra, take you, Stephen, for my lawful husband . . . to have and to hold." To have, to hold, to be held—thus we come to our sex chapter.

A marriage begins when bride and groom express their wedding vows. "However," writes John Paul II, "this sacramental word is . . . merely the sign of the coming into being of marriage. . . . The very words 'I take you as my wife—my husband' . . . can be fulfilled only by means of conjugal intercourse." Moving from the church to the bedroom, Audra and Stephen go from verbally expressing their willingness to become one flesh to actual physical union with each other.

"The love of man and woman is made holy in the sacrament of marriage," a prayer in the wedding liturgy declares. This does not mean merely that God gives Audra and Stephen his okay for sexual love when they say, "I do." It means that their love, including their lovemaking, is drawn into the love of Christ. Between the sheets, they celebrate Christ's presence in a uniquely intense way, and their lovemaking leads them deeper into Christ's love, which enriches and protects them.

To explore the holding and being held of marriage, we read from the Bible's collection of love songs, the Song of Solomon.

Week 3. "From this day forward, for better, for worse, for richer, for poorer, in sickness and in health."

After Paco and Maria initiate the sacrament at the altar and consummate it in bed, they live it out day by day in the kitchen, the office, the garage, the living room, the delivery room, the emergency room, the basketball court, the minivan, and who knows where else. In their comings and goings, stresses and strains, some days will be better than others. Facing challenges and, inevitably, hardships and suffering, each will need the other to be a faithful partner and companion. Will they be that for each other? Pushed to their limits, their flaws will be exposed. Will they be patient and forgiving? Will they grow in love? Our readings from Old and New Testament books focus our attention on these issues—and on God, the source of all help.

Week 4. "Will you, Gabriel and Nicole, accept children lovingly from God and bring them up according to the law of Christ and his Church?"

As far as begetting is concerned, there is an almost comic disproportion between cause and effect. A few minutes of yum-yum and voilà, Nicole and Gabriel are irrevocably changed: now they are parents forever. If they are committed to each other, their love will create the home their children need. But is any couple truly ready when baby heads down the birth canal and the moment comes for mom to push?

On the vast subject of parenting, our biblical readings offer a few guiding thoughts. Two prayers from the book of Psalms speak to us about relying on God; two excerpts from Proverbs speak about guiding our children into faithfulness to him.

Week 5. "Since it is your intention, Jason and LaTisha, to enter into marriage, declare your consent before God and his Church."

The family and friends gathered in church for the wedding are not there merely as a set of witnesses who can later affirm, "They really did go through with it." The assembly represents the whole Church. Jason and LaTisha get married *before* the Church because their marriage is to be lived *in* the Church.

Their marriage is not just for the bride and groom—or even just for themselves and their children. The nuptial blessing in the wedding ceremony speaks of the spouses being joined in order to "fulfill their mission in this world." The heart of this mission is expressed in the opening prayer of the wedding Mass, which asks God to make the couple "living witnesses to your divine love."

According to St. Paul in our reading in Week 1, husband and wife are a mirror of Christ and the Church. Well, Christ and the Church are at work in the world. If LaTisha and Jason are to be a sacrament—a sign and channel of Christ's love—*to* the world, they will have to be active *in* the world. Our readings from the Gospels and from St. Paul's letters help us reflect on this mission.

Week 6. "Shawn and Rebecca, may the peace of Christ live always in your hearts and in your home."

If Rebecca and Shawn are to find Christ in their lovemaking and child rearing, in their work and recreation, and in their joys and disappointments, they need to find him in themselves and in each other. They need to discern his presence, speak to him, and listen to him. The Scriptures and the wedding liturgy proclaim that Christ is present and accessible by his Spirit, especially in the Eucharist. Our final readings, from the Gospel of John, focus on Jesus' presence and spur us to reflect on ways in which we may deepen our relationship with him.

As will become clear in our readings, the Bible and the wedding liturgy strike distinctive notes on the subject of marriage. The biblical and liturgical perspective on marriage leads to wonder, even awe, at God's great plan. As male and female we are "fearfully and wonderfully made" (Psalm 139:14). This biblical view, which focuses our attention on God and his purposes, offers a refreshing corrective to any self-centered attitudes we may have.

The Bible and the liturgy set before us a purposeful picture of marriage. Marriage is for having children, for mutual help, for supporting each other in becoming holy, for sharing in Christ's mission in the world, and for companionship on the road home to God. These are noble purposes. Perhaps surprisingly, such great purposes are not a burden but a help. All of us have an unfortunate tendency to treat others as instruments for our own ends. Against this tendency, John Paul II points out, it is very useful to have a common purpose for which we can team up. Mutual love grows where there is a core of shared aspirations. If Liam and Tessa have common goals, they can focus their energies on working together to attain them, rather than pulling in opposite directions to accomplish separate agendas.

At the same time, alongside the wonder and high purposes of marriage, the Christian tradition is deeply conscious of the problem of sin. Scripture and the liturgy convey an awareness that the conflict between sin and redemption constitutes the field on which marriage is lived out. Our Old Testament readings in Week 1 focus on the positive: we are created "very good" by God (Genesis 1:31). If we had more than six weeks for our explorations, we could go on to read the biblical sequel, in which the first humans reject God and spiral downward into selfishness, exploitation, and violence (Genesis 3–11). Hardness of heart creeps into the relationship between husband and wife. All the aspects of marriage about which we will read in the coming weeks—joy and wonder, sex and friendship, child rearing, mission, spiritual life—are jeopardized by the selfishness and sin that are the opposite of love.

When Jesus quoted the creation accounts to affirm the permanence of marriage (Mark 10:6–9; Genesis 1:27; 2:24), he implied that he had come to heal spouses' hard-heartedness and to make faithful love between them possible again. He has brought an "outpouring of love in the new covenant of grace," the wedding liturgy declares. And this outpouring is "symbolized in the marriage covenant." In the sacrament of marriage, God's grace is available to husband and wife to help each turn away from self and toward the other. In fact, Christian marriage is a particular opportunity to experience this change of heart that Jesus offers everyone. Of course, spouses will experience a change of heart only by a constant reliance on Christ's help and struggle against sin.

The Bible and the liturgy encourage us to view marriage from an eternal perspective. A wedding blessing declares: "May daily problems never cause you undue anxiety, nor the desire for earthly possessions dominate your lives. But may your hearts' first desire be always the good things waiting for you in the life of heaven."

This perspective is crucial if spouses are to offer their time and talents to those in need. Our usual tendency is to narrow our care to those who are close to us. But love for God and a sense of our eternal destiny in him can outweigh our tendency to look inward and can free us to care for others who are in need. If husband and wife seek first the kingdom of God (Matthew 6:33), they will find some freedom from self-concern. Love for heaven and love for the afflicted are actually quite closely connected.

Above all, Scripture and liturgy sound the keynote for marriage in a single word: love. A prayer in the liturgy declares: "Love is man's origin, love is his constant calling, love is his fulfillment in heaven." Over the next six weeks, our biblical readings will ring the changes on the theme of love. Of course, it is easier to read about love than to love. But we will be reading God's words, and they have power to reshape our minds and hearts.

An important aspect of our subject will remain unexplored in our readings and reflections. Our focus of attention will be on the fact that God has designed us for marriage by creating us male and female. By doing so, he has given us a capacity for self-giving, for union with another person. This is, ultimately, a capacity for relationship with God. We will attain this goal at the resurrection, when, in risen bodies, we enter into union with God (see 1 Corinthians 6:13–14; 15:20–28). The part of this picture to which we will not devote attention in this guide concerns the fact that now, even in earthly life, Christ makes it possible to begin to experience this union with God in lifelong celibacy (see Matthew 19:11–12). The celibate person directs his or her human capacity for total self-giving toward God in a manner that leaves sexual activity aside but activates all the personal powers of love and devotion that are present in their human masculinity or femininity. In a sense, the celibate person takes God as spouse.

While marriage is a great sacrament, leading the spouses to God, the Catholic tradition has always considered celibacy for the "kingdom of heaven" (Matthew 19:12) as a kind of shorter, steeper road of personal transformation toward union with God (1 Corinthians 7:25–35). This tradition is based on the practice of Jesus himself and on his call to those original disciples to whom the gift of celibacy was given. Happy are those who are called to this path of celibacy and walk on it! Nevertheless, celibacy is not our topic in this short book, and we will not be saying any more about it. In passing, however, it is worth observing that the Church does not commend celibacy by depreciating marriage. Rather, as St. John Chrysostom pointed out (he was a monk with a great appreciation for marriage), it is only when one sees how good marriage is that one can properly value the sacrifice involved in forgoing it.

Does this guide have anything to offer to those who are not married? We believe it does.

Those of us who are not married—for whatever reasons—can still appreciate the importance of marriage for our parents, relatives and friends, and for society as a whole. What Scripture says about marriage can help all of us to a better understanding of ourselves as men and women created to love and to serve. For those of us who are divorced or widowed, the Scripture readings can aid us in reflecting on our experience and can be a source of healing and instruction.

Discussion of marriage inevitably involves talking about children. Married couples who have not been able to have children sometimes find discussions of child rearing painful. But for those of us in this situation, the Scripture readings that touch on parenting may be a spur to prayer and to considering how we might put our parental abilities and resources to work for the good of children and others in need.

Each week the "Questions for Discussion" are divided into two sections. In the first section—"Questions for All"—you will find questions that are useful for anyone using the guide. The second section—"Questions for Spouses"—contains questions designed specifically to aid husbands and wives to reflect on their marriage.

Weddings are beautiful because marriage reflects the beauty of God and is a path toward God. As we begin, our prayer for every Joe and Millie, Khalil and Manal, Mike and Dianne who may use this book is that your reading of Scripture may lead you to a beautiful marriage by leading you to the beauty of Christ.

To Love and to Honor

Questions to Begin

10 minutes
Use a question or two to get warmed up for the reading. Couples: try to guess your spouse's answers.

1 What's your favorite love song or love poem?

2 As a child, what was the first thing you were ever put in charge of or told to take care of?

**Lord, grant that as they begin to live this sacrament
they may share with each other the gifts of your love
and become one in heart and mind
as witnesses to your presence in their marriage.**

Wedding Mass, Nuptial Blessing

Opening the Bible

*10 minutes
Read the passage aloud. Let individuals take turns reading
paragraphs.*

The Background

To get a basic understanding of marriage, we go to the beginning of
the Bible, to the book of Genesis, and read about the creation of
the human race. The Bible actually contains two creation accounts.
Each highlights particular aspects of God's purposes for marriage.

In the first account, God creates everything in six days,
then rests on the seventh. As our excerpt begins, the sixth day has
just dawned. Most of creation is already in place. The moment has
come for God's greatest display of creativity: us!

The second creation account puts events in a different
sequence. First God creates a man, then a garden and animals for
him. Last and certainly not least—indeed, as the high point of the
story—he creates a woman.

Our third reading comes from St. Paul's letter to the
Christians in Ephesus. Paul cites the second creation account to
shed light on Christ's relationship with the Church. Paul then uses
Christ's relationship with the Church to shed light on marriage.

The readings bear the marks of their authors' ancient
cultures. The Genesis authors display prescientific thinking about
the nature of the universe. St. Paul reflects first-century patriarchal
culture, which assumed that the husband holds authority over his
wife. God worked through the biblical writers without erasing all
their cultural assumptions—just as he works with us today. This
means that, as readers, we have a twofold task: first, to understand
what the sacred authors were saying to the people of their time;
and second, to disentangle their message from their cultural
assumptions in order to grasp their message for us today.

For some of us, Paul's call to wives to be submissive to
their husbands is a stumbling block to getting any benefit from
his instructions. The "Exploring the Theme" section on page 19
comments on this issue, and there is a further investigation in the
"Between Discussions" section on page 26.

The Reading: Genesis 1:26–31; 2:4–10, 15–25; Ephesians 4:1–2; 5:1–2, 21–33

Creation Story One

Genesis 1:26 . . . God said, "Let us make humankind in our image, according to our likeness; and let them have dominion over the fish of the sea, and over the birds of the air, and over the cattle, and over all the wild animals of the earth, and over every creeping thing that creeps upon the earth."

27 So God created humankind in his image,
in the image of God he created them;
male and female he created them.

28 God blessed them, and God said to them, "Be fruitful and multiply, and fill the earth and subdue it; and have dominion over the fish of the sea and over the birds of the air and over every living thing that moves upon the earth." . . . 30 . . . And it was so. 31 God saw everything that he had made, and indeed, it was very good.

Creation Story Two

Genesis 2:4 . . . In the day that the LORD God made the earth and the heavens, 5 when no plant of the field was yet in the earth and no herb of the field had yet sprung up—for the LORD God had not caused it to rain upon the earth, and there was no one to till the ground; 6 but a stream would rise from the earth, and water the whole face of the ground— 7 then the LORD God formed man from the dust of the ground, and breathed into his nostrils the breath of life; and the man became a living being.

8 And the LORD God planted a garden in Eden, in the east; and there he put the man whom he had formed. 9 Out of the ground the LORD God made to grow every tree that is pleasant to the sight and good for food, the tree of life also in the midst of the garden, and the tree of the knowledge of good and evil. 10 A river flows out of Eden to water the garden, and from there it divides and becomes four branches. . . .

15 The LORD God took the man and put him in the garden of Eden to till it and keep it. 16 And the LORD God commanded the man, "You may freely eat of every tree of the garden; 17 but of the

tree of the knowledge of good and evil you shall not eat, for in the day that you eat of it you shall die."

18 Then the LORD God said, "It is not good that the man should be alone; I will make him a helper as his partner." 19 So out of the ground the LORD God formed every animal of the field and every bird of the air, and brought them to the man to see what he would call them; and whatever the man called every living creature, that was its name. 20 The man gave names to all cattle, and to the birds of the air, and to every animal of the field; but for the man there was not found a helper as his partner.

21 So the LORD God caused a deep sleep to fall upon the man, and he slept; then he took one of his ribs and closed up its place with flesh. 22 And the rib that the LORD God had taken from the man he made into a woman and brought her to the man. 23 Then the man said,

> "This at last is bone of my bones
>   and flesh of my flesh;
> this one shall be called Woman,
>   for out of Man this one was taken."

24 Therefore a man leaves his father and his mother and clings to his wife, and they become one flesh. 25 And the man and his wife were both naked, and were not ashamed.

Christian Life and Christian Marriage

Ephesians 4:1 I . . . beg you to lead a life worthy of the calling to which you have been called, 2 with all humility and gentleness, with patience, bearing with one another in love. . . . 5:1 . . . [B]e imitators of God, as beloved children, 2 and live in love, as Christ loved us and gave himself up for us, a fragrant offering and sacrifice to God. . . .

21 Be subject to one another out of reverence for Christ.

22 Wives, be subject to your husbands as you are to the Lord. 23 For the husband is the head of the wife just as Christ is the head of the church, the body of which he is the Savior. 24 Just as the church is subject to Christ, so also wives ought to be, in everything, to their husbands.

25 Husbands, love your wives, just as Christ loved the church and gave himself up for her, 26 in order to make her holy by cleansing her with the washing of water by the word, 27 so as to present the

church to himself in splendor, without a spot or wrinkle or anything of the kind—yes, so that she may be holy and without blemish. [28] In the same way, husbands should love their wives as they do their own bodies. He who loves his wife loves himself. [29] For no one ever hates his own body, but he nourishes and tenderly cares for it, just as Christ does for the church, [30] because we are members of his body.

[31] "For this reason a man will leave his father and mother and be joined to his wife, and the two will become one flesh." [32] This is a great mystery, and I am applying it to Christ and the church. [33] Each of you, however, should love his wife as himself, and a wife should respect her husband.

First Impression

5 minutes
Briefly mention a question you have about the reading or one thing in it that surprised, impressed, delighted, or challenged you. No discussion! Just listen to one another's reactions.

Exploring the Theme

If participants have not read this section already, read it aloud.
Otherwise go on to "Questions for Reflection and Discussion."

Genesis 1:26–31. Ancient Near Eastern people regarded their kings as images and representatives of the gods. In the biblical authors' view, God's likeness is seen not only in the king on his throne but in every guy plowing his field and every gal leading her goats up the hillside. *All* humans bear God's image. Each of us is a member of the royal family, the human race, which God has created to rule the earth for him.

Masculinity and femininity are dimensions of our likeness to God. God has no sex, but by making us male and female he enables us to be life givers, like him. As men and women, we can cooperate with him in giving life to children, who also bear the divine image (see Genesis 4:1; 5:1–3). God's first words to the human race (1:28) make our assignment clear: Fill the earth with children!

Genesis 2:4–10, 15–25. The first creation account viewed us as a group: "in the image of God he created them" (Genesis 1:27). The second account views us as individuals. The process by which God brings the first human into existence— carefully shaping the body, then breathing life into the nose— strikingly symbolizes God's desire for a face-to-face relationship with this creature. Despite the nearness of God, however, the human creature lacks something. The creator himself declares that the man's aloneness is not good. By himself, the man cannot fulfill the purpose for which he is created. He is designed to live with another.

What kind of other does he need? God expresses the criteria: "a helper as his partner" (2:18). The Hebrew word translated "helper" means "a support in the necessities of life." The word does not have servile connotations. In the Old Testament, it is applied most often to God, as when the psalmist cries out: "Hasten to me, O God! You are my *help* and my deliverer" (Psalm 70:5, emphasis added; also Psalm 121:1–2). "Partner" translates a word meaning "in the presence of," "over against," "opposite to," "corresponding to." It denotes a counterpart, and thus an equal. In the context of the story, it means a sexual complement.

So God creates woman. From the entire ancient Near East, this is the only account known in which the creation of woman features as an event in its own right, distinct from the creation of man. Thus, simply by its presence, the account underlines her equality with the man.

One may wonder whether the man had known exactly what he was looking for, but he sure knows it when he sees it. As the man catches sight of the woman, we hear the human voice for the first time in Scripture—and it speaks poetry, indeed, love poetry. *This one,* the man declares, is a fitting partner (2:23)! The woman corresponds to the man and the man to the woman in a delightful way.

Up to this point, the narrator has referred to the man with the Hebrew word for "human being" or "mankind." Now the man refers to himself with the Hebrew word meaning "adult male." "This one shall be called Woman, for out of *Man* this one was taken" (2:23; emphasis added). Biblical scholar Nahum M. Sarna remarks: "He discovers his own manhood and fulfillment only when he faces the woman, the human being who is to be his partner in life." What does the woman discover as she looks at the man? The (presumably male) author leaves us guessing.

In a figurative way, the account communicates a profound message about the mutual attraction of man and woman. Viewed against the background of this story of God's taking woman out of man, men's and women's desires for each other appear as a longing for a lost unity. Desire for completion in mutual love, the story indicates, has been inscribed in the depths of our being. As men and women, we are designed for the union in which two "become one flesh" (2:24). As John Paul II puts it, the human body has a "spousal meaning." We are made for marriage.

While the first creation story viewed our sexual difference as a capacity for cooperating with God in creating new human beings, the second account looks at our sexual difference as the basis for partnership and joy. And with this focus, the story draws to a close. At the fade-out (2:25), the man and the woman are "in the presence of" and "over against" each other, gazing in wonder at the helper-partner-lover-friend who has suddenly appeared.

We might wonder what happened to the concept of our being created in "the image of God" (1:27) in the second account. The concept is not mentioned explicitly, yet it is present implicitly. Commenting on the second account, John Paul II writes that, united in love, the man and woman become "an image of an inscrutable divine communion of persons"—the Father, Son, and Holy Spirit. In addition, John Paul II writes, by their love for each other, husband and wife reflect God's covenant love for the human race. For this reason, he calls marriage the "primordial sacrament."

Ephesians 4:1–2; 5:1–2, 21. Before speaking specifically to wives and husbands, Paul appeals to all Christians to love one another as Christ has loved all. The "humility" that Paul recommends (4:2) means considering others to be deserving of our care, putting their needs ahead of our own. (Paul points to Jesus as the perfect example of humility in Philippians 2:3–8.) To the extent that humility means acting as a servant of others, it means subordinating ourselves to them. Thus, Paul's words "be subject to one another out of reverence for Christ" (5:21) mean that we should serve one another humbly and lovingly. As Paul writes elsewhere: "Through love become slaves to one another" (Galatians 5:13). This is the essence of Christian living, and thus of married life.

But 5:21 is not only the conclusion of Paul's appeal to all Christians to live in love; it is also the beginning of his instructions concerning relationships in which, in the first-century household, one party was expected to submit to the authority of another: wives to husbands, children to parents, slaves to masters (5:22–6:9). Thus, 5:21 prepares the way for Paul's call to wives to be subordinate to their husbands. As we will see, however, Paul modifies his instruction to spouses in a way that shifts the center of attention away from authority and toward mutual love.

Ephesians 5:22–33. Paul explains that the second creation account (Genesis 2:21–25) contains a hidden meaning: it is a kind of parable for the relationship between Christ and the Church. As God brought forth Eve from Adam's body, he brought the Church into existence from the body of Jesus when he gave himself up to death on the cross (Ephesians 2:11–22). The marital imagery highlights Jesus' desire to be united with us: he loves us in a way that resembles Adam's desire to be "one flesh" with Eve (5:31).

Before Christ came, his marriage with the Church was foreshadowed in the marriage of Adam and Eve. Now that Christ has come, his marriage with the Church is reflected in every marriage among his followers. The spouses are joined in the love of Christ, who lives in them. Thus, Christian marriage is a sacrament—an earthly reality through which Christ shows his love.

While Paul calls husbands to "love your wives" (5:25), he does not explicitly tell wives to "love" their husbands. Nevertheless, his call to wives to be subordinate to their husbands implies a call to love, for his call to all Christians to show humble, serving love (4:1–2; 5:1–2, 21) echoes here in his instructions to spouses. And, while Paul tells wives, not husbands, to "be subject" (5:22), he implicitly calls husbands to subordinate themselves to their wives, for loving their wives means subordinating themselves to their wives' welfare. "Love makes the husband simultaneously subject to the wife," John Paul II observes, "just as the wife to the husband." Their gift of self to each other, John Paul II says, "is also a mutual subjection." Of course, the model of this kind of subordination in humble love is Jesus.

Reflections. We humans are most remarkable creatures: we bear a likeness to God. And, since marriage is the "primordial sacrament," that is a sign of God's love for the human race, married couples bear God's image in a special way. In addition, Christian married couples are a special reflection of Christ's saving love. How awesome!

Equally awesome is the response to all this that spouses are called to make. Is anyone capable of living out Paul's vision of marriage as a relationship of total, self-giving love? New Testament scholar Stephen Miletic suggests that spouses take Paul's words as a challenge—as though Paul were saying: "Respond to the summons to love one another—and discover whether Christ will supply the love you need!"

Questions for Reflection and Discussion

45 minutes
Choose questions according to your interest and time.

Questions for All

1 Reread Genesis 2:21–22. What was the man doing when the woman first caught sight of him?

2 Can you detect a similarity between God's view of creation in Genesis 1:31 and the view of Eve that Adam expresses in 2:23? If so, what might be the significance of the similarity?

3 What does it mean for spouses to be companions in life? Should spouses be friends? What does friendship in marriage mean? Is there a difference between the friendship of spouses and other friendships?

4 In what ways does a man come to know himself—and a woman to know herself—more deeply through marriage?

Questions for Spouses

5 Offer an example or two of spouses loving each other by humbly serving each other. What can you learn from their example? What step could you take to love your spouse better?

6 What do you appreciate about your spouse? How do you express your appreciation? In what ways has your appreciation of your spouse faded? What could be done to bring it back to life?

7 For personal reflection: Do you ever think of your spouse as an image of God? What change in how you relate to your spouse might you make from reflecting on this reality?

8 For personal reflection: Have you ever written a love poem for your spouse—or composed a song, made a drawing or painting or photograph, planted or arranged flowers for him or her? What creative expression of appreciation could you offer your spouse sometime soon?

9 **Focus question.** Tell each other something you appreciate about the other. Discuss ways that spouses can express their appreciation of each other. Are some ways more important for men? for women? What expressions of appreciation by your spouse do you especially value?

10 minutes
Use one of these approaches—or create your own!

♦ Read aloud this blessing of St. Paul in his letter to the Ephesians (1:17–19):

I pray that the God of our Lord Jesus Christ, the Father of glory, may give you a spirit of wisdom and revelation as you come to know him, so that, with the eyes of your heart enlightened, you may know what is the hope to which he has called you, what are the riches of his glorious inheritance among the saints, and what is the immeasurable greatness of his power for us who believe, according to the working of his great power.

Take a few minutes for reflection on the presence of Christ in your marriage—or, if you are not married, on your life as a whole. End together with an Our Father.

♦ "Realization of the value of the gift awakens the need to show gratitude," writes John Paul II, on the mutual gift of man and woman in marriage. In your own words, express your gratitude to God for your spouse and your marriage—or for God's gift of marriage to the human race. Close with an Our Father.

Between Discussions

Being Subordinate to One Another
A Further Look at Ephesians 5

Our reading from Ephesians raises the issue of husbands
having authority over their wives. St. Paul's words deserve
careful examination.

In the ancient world, pagan, Jewish, and Christian
thinkers gave instructions to household members concerning
their relationships with each other. These instructions commonly
addressed spouses, parents and children, and masters and
household slaves. The New Testament contains several examples
that reflect both the gospel spirit of humility and love and the
authoritarian, patriarchal culture of the time (Colossians 3:18–4:1;
1 Peter 3:1–7). In Ephesians 5, Paul seems to have drawn on an
existing set of instructions but expanded the section directed to
husbands and wives.

In the material he has added, Paul shows the connection
between Christian marriage and Christ's relationship with the
Church. Christ, says Paul, is the model for the husband; because
as Christ is "head" of the Church, the husband is "head" of his wife
(5:23). But what does Paul mean by "head"?

In Paul's language, Greek, the term *head,* used figuratively,
might refer to *authority* (as when we refer to someone as the head
of an organization) or *source* (as when we speak of the headwaters
of a river). In determining which meaning Paul has in mind here, it
is important to note that Paul also speaks of Christ as "the Savior"
of his body, the Church (5:23). Since "savior" means "protector
and sustainer of life," this reference indicates that Paul is mainly
thinking of Christ as source of life rather than exerciser of authority.
This fits with Paul's picture of Christ elsewhere in the letter. Earlier,
he spoke of Christ as head of the Church in the sense of his being
its source of life and power, its provider of the gifts and graces it
needs to function as his body in the world (4:7–16). Obviously, Paul
also acknowledges Christ as head of the Church in the sense of
being its supreme authority. He is the Church's "one Lord" (4:5).
But, in Ephesians, Paul does not show Christ exercising his authority
over the Church by giving it directions for particular situations or
sitting in judgment over it. Nor does Paul portray the Church's
relationship with Christ as consisting essentially in following his
directions. Rather, Paul points to Christ as the source of the

Church's life, and encourages the Church to receive Christ's life, to imitate his example, and to share in his mission (1–2; 6:10–20). Thus, it is primarily Christ as life giver rather than Christ as ruler that Paul seems to have in mind when he says that the husband is the head of his wife as Christ is the head of the Church.

But what can it mean for the husband to be the source of life for his wife? Christ is the unique source of life for all. The husband is not a source of life. He is no one's savior.

Paul seems to mean that the husband is to become a sign for his wife of Christ's life-giving love. Christ is the savior; the husband is to share in Christ's saving intentions for his wife. The husband is to commit himself to Christ's saving purpose for his wife, to aim at her salvation, her spiritual welfare, her eternal good. Christ has given his life to bring the Church to life and "make her holy" (5:25–26). A husband who truly shares in Christ's life-giving headship will want his wife to experience Christ's saving love.

Notice that the ultimate focus is not on the husband but on Christ. Christ lavishes good on the Church so that the Church may be beautiful for himself. The husband is to imitate Christ by lavishing good on his wife—not so that she may be beautiful for the *husband* but so that she might be beautiful for *Christ.*

By focusing on Christ's life-giving headship as the model for the husband, and by exhorting the husband to love his wife "as Christ loved the church" (5:25–33), Paul shifts the husband's attention away from exercising authority. His exhortation to husbands is similar to Jesus' response to his disciples who wanted him to appoint them to positions of authority. Without denying the existence of authority in the Church, Jesus impressed on them the importance of adopting an attitude of service (Mark 10:42–45; see also John 13:1–17).

Remarkably, Paul does not encourage husbands to exercise authority over their wives. "What we know about the ancient world would lead us to believe that husbands would have the right to enforce submission if it was not voluntarily offered," writes New Testament scholar Ernest Best. Yet Paul does not advise husbands to do so. In fact, Paul emphasizes the husband's duty to love his wife. This was not the sort of thing first-century husbands were used to hearing.

Paul envisions mutual love between the spouses, even though his appeals to husbands and to wives are not identical. He tells husbands to love their wives—and any husband who does love his wife will subordinate himself to her in the sense of putting her welfare before his own. And his instruction to wives to subordinate themselves to their husbands is, in a Christian context, a call to imitate Christ's humble, serving love.

Nevertheless, Paul does affirm the husband's authority over the wife by urging wives to subordinate themselves to their husbands (5:22, 24, 33). It must be asked whether there isn't a contradiction between this support for patriarchy and his summons to mutual love. It did not seem so to Paul and his first Christian readers, who shared the outlook of their patriarchal society. And for believers during most of Christian history, who also lived in patriarchal societies, the concept of mutual love between the spouses seemed to blend well with the concept of the husband's authority. From Church Fathers such as Tertullian (second century) and St. John Chrysostom (fourth century) to Pope Pius XI (early twentieth century), Christian teachers appealed to spouses to love each other tenderly, while also insisting that wives should obey their husbands. In the last half century, however, as patriarchal assumptions have ebbed in Western societies, the relationship between Paul's patriarchal view of marriage and his call to mutual love has been reexamined.

Recent Christian thinkers have distinguished what is old from what is new in Paul's teaching. John Paul II, for example, in his letter *On the Dignity and Vocation of Women,* regards Paul's exhortation to wives ("be subject to your husbands as you are to the Lord. For the husband is the head of the wife"—5:22–23) as a "way of speaking . . . profoundly rooted in the customs and religious tradition of the time." According to this "old" ethos, submission in marriage is a one-way street—wife to husband—just as the submission of the Church to Christ is a one-way street. But Christ has brought a "new" ethos, the pope writes. "The challenge presented by the 'ethos' of the redemption," John Paul says, "is clear and definitive. All the reasons in favor of the 'subjection' of woman to man in marriage must be understood in the sense of a 'mutual subjection' of both 'out of reverence for Christ.'" John Paul II believes that Paul basically presents this new ethos in Ephesians 5, even while continuing to some degree to "communicate what is 'old,'" as in Ephesians 5:22–24.

"The apostolic letters are addressed to people living in an environment marked by that same traditional way of thinking and acting," the pope writes. "The 'innovation' of Christ is a fact: it constitutes the unambiguous content of the evangelical message and is the result of the Redemption. However, the awareness that in marriage there is mutual 'subjection of the spouses out of reverence for Christ,' and not just that of the wife to the husband, must gradually establish itself in hearts, consciences, behavior and customs." If the call has taken a long time to find acceptance, the pope urges us not to become discouraged. Remember, he says, that the New Testament writers also undercut the foundations of slavery by declaring that "'in Christ Jesus . . . there is no more . . . slave or freeman.' Yet how many generations were needed for such a principle to be realized in the history of humanity through the abolition of slavery!"

An indication of the shift in thinking about Paul's teaching can be seen from a comparison of the new *Catechism of the Catholic Church* (1997) with the preceding *Roman Catechism* (1566). *The Roman Catechism* stated both the call to mutual love between spouses and the subordination of wife to husband, quoting the appeal to wives to obey their husbands in 1 Peter 3:1–6 (section 2.7.26–27). The new *Catechism* says nothing about wives being subordinate to their husbands. It does not quote 1 Peter 3:1–6. In fact, perhaps to avoid misunderstanding, it never quotes Ephesians 5:22–24, 33—the verses that call wives to be subordinate to their husbands—or even mentions them in a footnote.

To Have and to Hold

Questions to Begin

10 minutes
Use a question or two to get warmed up for the reading. Couples: try to guess your spouse's answers.

1 What's your favorite love story?

2 How would you describe yourself?
- ❏ I'm an over-the-top romantic.
- ❏ I like a good love story now and then.
- ❏ My friends tell me I'm not very sentimental.
- ❏ I'm a flinty realist with no patience for romantic flutterings.

Christ abundantly blesses this love.

Wedding Mass, Introductory Address

Opening th

10 minutes
Read the pas_____ud. Let individuals take turns reading
paragraphs. Su_____tion for couples: husband, read the groom's
parts; wife, read ___e bride's parts.

The Background

Adam's poetic *wow* on meeting Eve (Genesis 2:23) is not the only love poetry in the Bible. The Old Testament contains a collection of love poems, called the Song of Solomon—sometimes called the Song of Songs, meaning "the most beautiful of all songs." John Paul II points out the connection between Adam's outburst and the Song. What the first man expressed in "just a few simple and essential words," John Paul II says, "is developed here in a full dialogue, or rather in a duet, in which the groom's words are interwoven with the bride's and they complement each other." In Genesis, "on seeing the woman created by God, man's first words express wonder and admiration, even more, the sense of fascination. . . . *A similar fascination* . . . runs in fuller form through the verses of the Song of Songs."

In addition to romantic love, the Song has often been thought to express the love between God and the people of Israel, and between Christ and the individual human heart. As poetry, it lends itself to these additional levels of interpretation. But whatever additional meanings the Song may have, it does not cease to be an expression of love between a man and a woman. As romantic poetry, it is God's word to us. This is how John Paul II interpreted the Song in a series of talks he gave on married love in the 1970s, and it is the way we will read it here.

The question of the Song's connection with Solomon, king of Israel, is debated by scholars but need not concern us here. The identity of the Song's lovers is also mysterious. Without exploring this complex issue, it is possible to state that the love songs can be understood, as the pope says, as a duet between a bride (Song 4:9) and a groom. A tidbit of information: Lebanon is mentioned in the Song because of its proverbially lush vegetation.

The Song is a rich source of reflection on the erotic dimension of marriage. It would be a mistake, however, to treat the Song like a textbook. This is *poetry*. The route to any lessons to be learned lies through enjoyment of the beauty. The lovers are enchanted by each other. Put analytical thinking on hold and feel their enchantment.

The Reading: Song of Solomon 3:1–4; 4:9–5:1; 7:6–12; 8:6–7

The Bride

3:1 Upon my bed at night
I sought him whom my soul loves;
I sought him, but found him not;
I called him, but he gave no answer.
2 "I will rise now and go about the city,
in the streets and in the squares;
I will seek him whom my soul loves."
I sought him, but found him not.
3 The sentinels found me,
as they went about in the city.
"Have you seen him whom my soul loves?"

4 Scarcely had I passed them,
when I found him whom my soul loves.
I held him, and would not let him go. . . .

The Groom

4:9 You have ravished my heart, my sister, my bride,
you have ravished my heart with a glance of your eyes,
with one jewel of your necklace.
10 How sweet is your love, my sister, my bride!
how much better is your love than wine,
and the fragrance of your oils than any spice!
11 Your lips distill nectar, my bride;
honey and milk are under your tongue;
the scent of your garments is like the scent of
Lebanon.
12 A garden locked is my sister, my bride,
a garden locked, a fountain sealed.
13 Your channel is an orchard of pomegranates
with all choicest fruits,
henna with nard,
14 nard and saffron, calamus and cinnamon,
with all trees of frankincense,

    myrrh and aloes,
        with all chief spices—
15 a garden fountain, a well of living water,
        and flowing streams from Lebanon.

16 Awake, O north wind,
        and come, O south wind!
Blow upon my garden
        that its fragrance may be wafted abroad.

The Bride

4:16 Let my beloved come to his garden,
        and eat its choicest fruits.

The Groom

5:1 I come to my garden, my sister, my bride;
        I gather my myrrh with my spice,
        I eat my honeycomb with my honey,
        I drink my wine with my milk. . . .

7:6 How fair and pleasant you are,
        O loved one, delectable maiden!
7 You are stately as a palm tree,
        and your breasts are like its clusters.
8 I say I will climb the palm tree
        and lay hold of its branches.
Oh, may your breasts be like clusters of the vine,
        and the scent of your breath like apples,
9 and your kisses like the best wine. . . .

The Bride

7:10 I am my beloved's,
        and his desire is for me.
11 Come, my beloved,
        let us go forth into the fields,
        and lodge in the villages;

12 let us go out early to the vineyards,
    and see whether the vines have budded,
whether the grape blossoms have opened
    and the pomegranates are in bloom.
There I will give you my love. . . .

8:6 Set me as a seal upon your heart,
    as a seal upon your arm;
for love is strong as death,
    passion fierce as the grave.
Its flashes are flashes of fire,
    a raging flame.
7 Many waters cannot quench love,
    neither can floods drown it.
If one offered for love
    all the wealth of his house,
    it would be utterly scorned.

First Impression

5 minutes
*Briefly mention a question you have about the reading or one
thing in it that surprised, impressed, delighted, or challenged
you. No discussion! Just listen to one another's reactions.*

If participants have not read this section already, read it aloud.
Otherwise go on to "Questions for Reflection and Discussion."

3:1–4. The Bride. When the Song was written, it was
socially unacceptable for a woman to be out on the streets at
night by herself, so we should probably interpret the bride's
nighttime searchings as a daydream. Her fantasizing reflects her
preoccupation—her heart's constant straining toward her beloved.
In her imagination, she makes the rounds of the city. When she runs
into night watchmen patrolling the streets, she makes no apology
for being out alone but asks if they have seen her lover! Love makes
her bold, one commentator remarks.

It is not the watchmen but the bride who takes someone
into custody. Catching sight of her beloved, she seizes him ("I held
him"—the Hebrew word can mean "arrest"). She loves him with all
her "soul"—the Hebrew word means her "whole being."

4:9–16. The Groom. The groom is as far gone on the
bride as she is on him. "You have ravished my heart," he complains
happily. The Hebrew verb means either "you have stolen my heart"
or "you make my heart beat faster." A good translation, one scholar
proposes, would be "You drive me crazy!"

The groom addresses the bride as "sister"—a figure of
speech expressing a feeling of intense closeness. While surprising
to modern ears, it is not so different from Adam's greeting of Eve
(Genesis 2:23), since "bone of my bones and flesh of my flesh" can
mean "my kinsman" or "my kinswoman" (see 2 Samuel 19:12; Tobit
5:21; 7:15).

"Your lips distill nectar" (4:11), the groom tells the bride;
in other words, her words are sweet, her lips are sweet, her breath
is sweet. She seems to him like a garden filled with fragrant plants.
The aromatic trees and shrubs named grow in places far apart in
the Middle East; no one garden could actually contain all of them.
Like the beloved's presence, this exotic garden exceeds ordinary,
everyday experience. The groom's description of his bride is discreet
but emphatically erotic; "channel," for example, is a metaphor for
her vagina. The Hebrew word for "orchard" (4:13) here gives us the
English word *paradise*—a hint that the lovers taste the joy that the
first man and woman experienced in the garden of Eden.

The man summons the winds to come and blow through the garden and release its fragrances. . . .

4:16. The Bride. ". . . Winds?" the woman responds. "Let my beloved himself come into his garden."

The image of the woman as "a garden locked, a fountain sealed" (4:12), John Paul II remarks, expresses the woman's self-possession: she is "master of her own mystery." As "master of her own choice," the bride freely opens herself to her beloved.

5:1; 7:6–9. The Groom. To her lover, the woman seems like a stately date palm tree. The groom does not mean she is thin; he is expressing the impression her breasts make on him: they loom as prominent as the heavy clusters of dates at the top of a palm's slender trunk.

7:10–12; 8:6–7. The Bride. The woman suggests a weekend in the country, where the pair can be alone. There is something private about their love, which seeks to withdraw from others' eyes and pushes practical considerations into the background. Remarkably absent from the Song are any references to fathers, property, inheritance, dowry, bride-price—the factors that shaped marriage in the ancient world. The Song is about the lovers. Not even children are mentioned.

The bride uses a rare Hebrew word in speaking about her beloved's "desire." Almost the only other appearance of this word in the Bible is when God tells Eve that, in punishment for her disobedience, her "desire" will be for her husband—a situation that will expose her to domination by him (Genesis 3:16). The bride's affirmation that her *beloved's* "desire" (7:10) is for *her* implies that their love for one another is mutual. Love has lifted the curse of domination; equality between man and woman is restored. In a sense, by love, the pair have found their way back to paradise.

"Set me as a seal upon your heart" (8:6). In the ancient Near East, a person might carry a seal—a small stone incised with his or her name, used for signing documents by impressing the name on a lump of soft clay. Because seals commonly contained symbols and pictures of gods, they were regarded as amulets and were worn on a necklace or bracelet to ward off evil. The woman expresses her wish to be an amulet on her beloved's chest and arm. "Love is strong as death" (8:6), she declares. She is not claiming that her love can prevent the groom from ever dying. Her statement is a way of saying that her love is exceedingly strong. Compare our way of using the word *dead* in English to mean "absolutely," as in the expression *dead wrong*. We might say that the woman is declaring that her love is "dead strong": nothing is stronger. The amulet imagery speaks of her desire to put herself between her beloved and any danger. She *would* save him from death if she could. Such "passion," such devotion, is priceless (8:6–7).

Erotic love, as we all know, can descend into self-seeking and exploitation. Yet it does not have that effect on the lovers in the Song. Their fascination and desire leads them upward into honoring, cherishing, and commitment. The Song invites us to ponder why their love has this upward trend.

Reflections. The bride and groom sing to each other with frank eroticism, yet their poetry contains no obscene descriptions of body parts or sexual intercourse. Rather, their figurative language expresses the overpowering impression that each makes on the other. They celebrate their longing for each other, their enjoyment of each other's manliness and femininity, their intoxication with each other's presence. Biblical scholar Othmar Keel describes the lovers this way: "The basis of love in the Song is a great admiration of the beloved partner, who seems unapproachable in his or her radiance—distant on inaccessible mountains, hidden in locked gardens, painfully longed for and sought. The lovers mutually experience one another as so beautiful, so radiant, so magnificent that every discovery, every approach, every possession of the other can be experienced only as unfathomable gift." In this, the Song's singers express something true of all lovers. Admittedly, few of us are paragons of physical beauty, to say the least. But every lover is struck somehow by the beloved's beauty, especially in the euphoric days of courtship and honeymoon.

The tendency to take rather than give operates in all personal relationships, but it is especially powerful where sex is involved, due to the strength of our desires. We are tempted to treat the other person as a means to our ends rather than as an end in himself or herself. Yet the Song alerts us to the possibility that sexual love also presents a unique opportunity for self-giving.

In fact, our human tendency to selfishness is not rooted in our sexual desire but in our will, which is flawed by what theologians call original sin (see Romans 5:12–21). As Genesis 2 shows, sexual desire reflects a natural need—a need that God has created in us. Since it reflects a God-given need, our sexual desire is not, in itself, selfish. John Paul II calls sex an "imbalance": man and woman need each other to complete their being. It is natural to desire completion, natural to want to share our whole life with one person—a person through whom we can attain the fulfillment of being a wife or husband, a father or mother. Since we are needy creatures, the pope observes, need and desire are present in all human love, even our love for God.

The Song suggests that sexual desire, far from being an obstacle to love, can play a crucial part in its growth. How can this happen? Perhaps we could describe it this way: Fascination draws the lover close to the beloved, and from this privileged, intimate vantage point, the lover glimpses a deeper beauty, the beloved's inherent splendor as a human person. This insight becomes a bridge on which the lover can cross over, stand beside the beloved, and affirm this enchanting creature as a person of infinite value. "Experiencing how good you are for me," the lover whispers to the beloved, "I have begun to see how good you are—and to desire *your* good. Delighting in your presence, I have come to desire *your* happiness. I want to be that one person through whom you have the happiness of becoming the person God created you to be as husband and father, wife and mother. To love you, to devote myself to your good, would be my greatest joy. Let me have that joy. Set me as a seal upon your heart."

"The raw material of love"—that's what John Paul II calls erotic attraction, acknowledging, of course, that it can also be the raw material of mutual destruction. The question posed to lovers is: What are you creating with *your* love?

Questions for Reflection and Discussion

45 minutes
Choose questions according to your interest and time.

Questions for All

1 Identify what can be seen, heard, smelled, tasted, and felt in the poems. What is most emphasized? least emphasized? Do you find the balance surprising?

2 What is the value of the lovers speaking to each other in a poetic way? Reread 3:1–4. Would her words have the same effect on the man if the woman simply said, "I think about you all the time"? Reread 4:9–16. Would it be the same if the groom just said, "Let's make love," and the bride said, "All right"?

3 Besides erotic love, what other kinds of natural desires, attractions, and fascinations can lead a person to understand the real value of something? to devote themselves to something worthwhile? to find a path of personal fulfillment? to be of service to other people?

4 What makes a person beautiful? What true and false ideas of personal beauty are prevalent in society today? How do popular ideas of beauty affect those who do not measure up to them? Are there hidden kinds of beauty that are rarely appreciated? What shapes your ideas of personal beauty?

Questions for Spouses

5   What are the differences between falling in love and growing in love? What are the connections? What decisions or actions are crucial if being in love is to grow into living in love?

6   Concerning their sexual desires, what kinds of things are helpful and appropriate for spouses to say to each other?

7   Think of a recent moment when you saw something beautiful about your spouse. Did you tell him or her?

8   For personal reflection: What do you find beautiful, handsome, attractive, or exciting about your spouse? How has your view of your spouse changed over time? Is it possible for a person to lose sight of what is beautiful in someone they love? Can the vision be restored?

9   **Focus question.** Do you think of yourselves as lovers? How important is it for spouses to be lovers? Do husbands and wives naturally stop being lovers once they get married? when they have been married for a while? when they become a mom and a dad? when they become a grandma and a grandpa?

Prayer to Close

10 minutes
Use this approach—or create your own!

♦ Read aloud Tobit 8:4–9. Without going into the whole story, it is enough to know that these verses describe a young couple on their wedding night. After the reading, pause for silent reflection, and express any thoughts to God that may have been prompted by this week's reading and discussion. End with an Our Father.

FOR BETTER, FOR WORSE

Questions to Begin

10 minutes
Use a question or two to get warmed up for the reading. Couples: try to guess your spouse's answers.

1 Mention an unexpected good thing that happened during the last week.

2 When was the last time you laughed?

Lord, may they both praise you when they are happy and turn to you in their sorrows.
May they be glad that you help them in their work and know that you are with them in their need.

Wedding Mass, Nuptial Blessing

Opening the Bible

10 minutes
*Read the passage aloud. Let individuals take turns reading para-
graphs. Suggestion for couples: read the passages from Romans
and 2 Corinthians twice, the second time substituting your own
names for "us" in Romans and for "we" in 2 Corinthians.*

The Background

Marriages may be made in heaven, but they are lived on earth,
where things often do not go as expected. Our first reading,
from the Old Testament book of Ecclesiastes, sets before us the
changeableness of life. It sounds a note of realism.

In our next two readings, St. Paul urges us to see the
difficulties of life in light of God's love for us. In his letters to the
Christians in Rome and Corinth, he presents a perspective on
life that goes beyond the vision of the author of Ecclesiastes. No
suffering that we may face can tear us from God's embrace. God
is not only with us in our vulnerabilities to life's sorrows; he makes
himself present in an especially powerful way in our weaknesses.
Christ can carry us through the rough times. This is bedrock on
which spouses can build a marriage.

Finally, from Paul's letter to the Colossians, we read about
the ever helpful qualities that can sustain spouses as they go
through all the times of their marriage, both good and bad.

The Reading: Ecclesiastes 3:1–11; Romans 8:28–39; 2 Corinthians 4:6–10, 16–17; Colossians 3:8–16

Life Has Its Ups and Downs

Ecclesiastes 3:1 For everything there is a season, and a time for every
matter under heaven:

> 2 a time to be born, and a time to die;
> a time to plant, and a time to pluck up what is planted;
> 3 a time to kill, and a time to heal;
> a time to break down, and a time to build up;
> 4 a time to weep, and a time to laugh;
> a time to mourn, and a time to dance;
> 5 a time to throw away stones, and a time to gather
> stones together;
> a time to embrace, and a time to refrain from
> embracing;

6 a time to seek, and a time to lose;
  a time to keep, and a time to throw away;
7 a time to tear, and a time to sew;
  a time to keep silence, and a time to speak;
8 a time to love, and a time to hate;
  a time for war, and a time for peace.

9 What gain have the workers from their toil? 10 I have seen the business that God has given to everyone to be busy with. 11 He has made everything suitable for its time; moreover he has put a sense of past and future into their minds, yet they cannot find out what God has done from the beginning to the end.

No Ups or Downs Can Separate Us from Christ

Romans 8:28 We know that all things work together for good for those who love God, who are called according to his purpose. 29 For those whom he foreknew he also predestined to be conformed to the image of his Son, in order that he might be the firstborn within a large family. . . .

31 What then are we to say about these things? If God is for us, who is against us? 32 He who did not withhold his own Son, but gave him up for all of us, will he not with him also give us everything else? 33 Who will bring any charge against God's elect? It is God who justifies. 34 Who is to condemn? It is Christ Jesus, who died, yes, who was raised, who is at the right hand of God, who indeed intercedes for us. 35 Who will separate us from the love of Christ? Will hardship, or distress, or persecution, or famine, or nakedness, or peril, or sword? . . . 37 No, in all these things we are more than conquerors through him who loved us. 38 For I am convinced that neither death, nor life, nor angels, nor rulers, nor things present, nor things to come, nor powers, 39 nor height, nor depth, nor anything else in all creation, will be able to separate us from the love of God in Christ Jesus our Lord.

2 Corinthians 4:6 . . . [I]t is the God who said, "Let light shine out of darkness," who has shone in our hearts to give the light of the knowledge of the glory of God in the face of Jesus Christ.

[7] But we have this treasure in clay jars, so that it may be made clear that this extraordinary power belongs to God and does not come from us. [8] We are afflicted in every way, but not crushed; perplexed, but not driven to despair; [9] persecuted, but not forsaken; struck down, but not destroyed; [10] always carrying in the body the death of Jesus, so that the life of Jesus may also be made visible in our bodies. . . .

[16] So we do not lose heart. Even though our outer nature is wasting away, our inner nature is being renewed day by day. [17] For this slight momentary affliction is preparing us for an eternal weight of glory beyond all measure. . . .

Staying Together through All the Ups and Downs

Colossians 3:8 . . . [N]ow you must get rid of all such things—anger, wrath, malice, slander, and abusive language from your mouth. [9] Do not lie to one another, seeing that you have stripped off the old self with its practices [10] and have clothed yourselves with the new self, which is being renewed in knowledge according to the image of its creator. . . .

[12] As God's chosen ones, holy and beloved, clothe yourselves with compassion, kindness, humility, meekness, and patience. [13] Bear with one another and, if anyone has a complaint against another, forgive each other; just as the Lord has forgiven you, so you also must forgive. [14] Above all, clothe yourselves with love, which binds everything together in perfect harmony.

[15] And let the peace of Christ rule in your hearts, to which indeed you were called in the one body. And be thankful. [16] Let the word of Christ dwell in you richly; teach and admonish one another in all wisdom; and with gratitude in your hearts sing psalms, hymns, and spiritual songs to God.

First Impression

5 minutes
Briefly mention a question you have about the reading or one thing in it that surprised, impressed, delighted, or challenged you. No discussion! Just listen to one another's reactions.

Exploring the Theme

If participants have not read this section already, read it aloud. Otherwise go on to "Questions for Reflection and Discussion."

Ecclesiastes 3:1–11. The author of the book of Ecclesiastes is a man of faith, but also something of a pessimist. He looks the deficiencies in life squarely in the face. Sure, there is happiness, he acknowledges; but there is also woe. He sketches life with a comprehensive list of items that encompasses everything from birth to death, from war to peace (3:2–8). Isn't this how life is, he seems to ask us—big plusses and big minuses, and very changeable?

Weddings stand on the positive side of the list: dancing, laughing, loving, embracing, preparing for those who will be born. But marriage is not all party and honeymoon. The contrasts inevitably make themselves present. Marriage does not change the human condition. The world remains the same. What changes is that two are now going through it as one (see Ecclesiastes 4:9–12).

The author emphasizes that God "has made everything suitable for its time" (3:11). But God has not given us access to his timing. We cannot see the picture of our lives in the great tapestry that he is weaving (3:11).

All this leads the author to ask: "What gain have the workers from their toil?" (3:9). What good are our efforts if building is inevitably followed by demolition and if you can't synchronize your construction work with God's timing?

Similar questions can arise in marriage. Parents can reach a point where they question whether all their hard work was worth it. Watching an adult child squander his or her life, one wonders what was the point of all the soccer coaching, the carpooling, the camping trips. God's purposes may seem especially opaque in times of suffering. A parent looking at a child in a hospital bed may ask, "Why would God allow *this*?" Usually, there is no satisfactory answer this side of eternity. Spiritual writers speak of a dark night of the soul in a person's relationship with God, when joys and consolations evaporate, leaving the person in a bleak, lonely wilderness. Marriages, too, can have dark nights. Ecclesiastes serves to remind us that spouses commit themselves to go together not only through the difficulties they can change but through the harder ones they can't.

Romans 8:28–39. St. Paul puts life's unknowns in a new framework. The musings of Ecclesiastes retain their validity. The timing and purposes for the ups and downs in our lives are hidden in God. But, Paul proclaims, we have hope in darkness, because God has revealed the goal: final union with him. Toward that goal, God is working in "all things"—in all the lights and darks mentioned in Ecclesiastes—on behalf of those who cooperate with him (8:28).

If this approach seems overly spiritual, it should be noted that Paul is no less a realist than the author of Ecclesiastes. He acknowledges that there is a time for suffering, a time for being persecuted, a time for facing death. For Paul, these were not hypothetical possibilities. His ministry was full of suffering (Acts; 2 Corinthians 11:23–33). But what, Paul asks, can separate us from the love of Christ?

And what, spouses could add, can separate them from each other, if they are joined in Christ's love? The answer: their own selfishness and sin, if they let it, but nothing else. Christ's love for us is a power that embraces us, and for this reason "we are more than conquerors through him who loved us" (8:37).

2 Corinthians 4:6–10, 16–17. Again Paul reminds us of life's goal: the "eternal weight of glory" that God prepares for us (4:17). In light of this "glory beyond all measure," any hardship along the way is a "slight momentary affliction" (4:17). However, while Paul invites us to adopt this way of evaluating suffering, he knows that some of the afflictions he calls "slight" are almost unendurable. Suffering can drive us to the brink of despair (4:8–9; see 1:8).

Yet, we have not only the hope of life with God to come, Paul says, but God's life within us here and now; not only a future "weight of glory" (4:17) but a present "treasure"—Christ in us (4:6–7). When disaster strikes, it is only natural to feel at a loss, unable to go on. But, Paul insists, we must not "lose heart" (4:16); we must not lose sight of the treasure of Christ in us—in husband and wife together, each married couple can affirm.

Paul sums up the sorrowful dimension of life in a grim line: "Our outer nature is wasting away" (4:16). Picture being exhausted by working two jobs, struggling on a tight budget, growing old, going on dialysis, getting confused. . . . Paul declared in Romans that "in all these things we are more than conquerors" (Romans 8:37). Certainly the wasting away of our outer nature seems to be the very *opposite* of conquering. Yet it *is* conquering, Paul maintains, if we hold on to the treasure, to Christ.

In the early days of romance, a lover may catch a glimpse of the divine treasure in the beloved's heart, may sense the glory to which God calls the other. As the years pass, and the beloved's outer nature wastes away, the vision of his or her summons into the divine glory can sustain the spouse's respect, even reverence.

Colossians 3:8–16. To those in whom "Christ is" (3:11), Paul offers a checklist of appropriate ways of relating to one another.

◆ *Love* (3:14). Paul means the kind of love that God has revealed in Jesus, who laid down his life for us (Mark 10:42–45).

◆ *Forgiveness* (3:13). This is crucial. But Paul is not talking about being a doormat or submitting to abuse. Notice that he also speaks about admonishing one another (3:16), which involves talking directly about problems.

◆ *Wisdom* (3:16). Common sense and knowledge of the other person are required if problems are to be dealt with constructively. For spouses this means learning to speak in ways most likely to get through to each other. Lying in bed late at night is probably not the best moment for Stuart to present Faye with his argument for a new austerity budget.

◆ *Forbearance* (3:13). At the beginning of marriage, the need to bear with one another might seem remote. Why would you have to be patient with such a wonderful person? In time, however, some of what seemed endearing may become irritating. Grant's tendency to hang loose was fun when he and Arlene were going out. Now that they live together, she would appreciate a higher level of organization.

◆ *Grateful worship* (3:15). Since all has been made through Christ, including ourselves and our marriages, we can offer all of it through him in thankfulness to the Father. For Paul, this is the center of Christian living.

Questions for Reflection and Discussion

45 minutes
Choose questions according to your interest and time.

Questions for All

1 Select one of the times listed in the reading from Ecclesiastes 3. What event in your life does it bring to mind?

2 In the readings from Romans and 2 Corinthians, what answer does Paul offer to the question posed in Ecclesiastes 3:9?

3 Doesn't losing heart (2 Corinthians 4:16) involve some kind of decision? Can you illustrate your view with an example from real life?

4 What kind of decision is involved in clothing oneself with love (Colossians 3:14)? What are some examples of this?

5 What does it mean to "be thankful" (Colossians 3:15) when one is in the kind of situation that Paul refers to in 2 Corinthians 4:8–10?

Questions for Spouses

6 Reread Romans 8:38–39 and 2 Corinthians 4:8–10. How is Christ found in times of suffering? How has this happened in the marriages of couples you know? in your own marriage? (If you're in a group, be careful about not betraying any confidences.)

7 Reread Colossians 3:15. What does it mean to make thanksgiving the center of a marriage?

8 For personal reflection: What things do you do or say that would tend to strengthen your spouse's trust in God? What things wear down your spouse's trust in God?

9 For personal reflection: What two things suggested by Paul's instructions in Colossians 3 could you do (more often) toward your spouse? What two things could you do less often?

10 **Focus question.** Give an example of how your parents or another couple you know faced a difficult situation. What positive lesson can be learned from how they approached it? How could this help you in your own marriage when you and your spouse face difficulties? What helps you have faith in God in trying times? How can you help remind each other of the perspective on life that Paul presents in Romans and 2 Corinthians? How can a husband and wife stay close to Christ—and to each other—in difficult times?

Prayer to Close

10 minutes
Use one of these approaches—or create your own!

◆ Take a few minutes to express to God your thanks for marriages and families that you know. End with an Our Father.

◆ Here is a suggestion for spouses, for individual use. Using the reading from Colossians and a little imagination, create a "Spouse's Examination of Conscience." Organize it as "Things I may need to ask my spouse's forgiveness for." Then reuse it as a list of "Things I may need to forgive my spouse for." A few ideas:
❑ Spreading anxiety
❑ Criticizing unnecessarily
❑ Making fun of my spouse in front of other people
❑ Breaking a promise
❑ Making a decision alone that should have involved us both
❑ Seeking the limelight
❑ Withholding praise or thanks
❑ Being grouchy
❑ Nagging
❑ Undercutting the other's relationship with the children
❑ Not pulling my weight
❑ Pretending not to hear or see
❑ Spending on the sly
❑ Deliberately being late

Discuss your list with Christ.

Saints in the Making

A Couple of New Saints

This section is a supplement for individual reading.

It was a milestone in the history of the Church—the first joint beatification of a husband and wife. On October 21, 2001, with three of their children in attendance in St. Peter's Square, John Paul II recognized Luigi and Maria Beltrame Quattrocchi as an outstanding married couple whose "fidelity to the gospel and heroic virtues were verified in their life as spouses and parents." In good times and in bad, including two world wars, they kept the light of faith burning and passed it on to others, the pope noted.

Not quite a century before, Maria and Luigi had spoken their marriage vows in the Basilica of St. Mary Major. He was an up-and-coming lawyer who would go on to a distinguished legal and civil service career; she was a well-bred Florentine with an interest in the arts and education. Their love was deep, and was nourished by their desire to grow closer to God together. Each morning, the couple attended Mass, then went their separate ways—"he to his work, I to my tasks," Maria wrote years later. "But each of us kept within ourselves a constant awareness of the other's presence." Whatever the difficulties, life was rich, filled with "the joy—always new—of being together."

Filippo, the Quattrocchis' first son, was born eleven months after the wedding. Stefania and Cesare followed in close succession. Then, in late 1913, Maria began hemorrhaging four months into her pregnancy. The baby was beyond rescue, a respected doctor told them, and even Maria had just a 5 percent chance of surviving *if* she had an abortion. Luigi and Maria exchanged a look, then turned their eyes to the crucifix on the wall. "No," they told the doctor. "But don't you realize," he said, addressing Luigi, "that by doing this you're certain to become a widower with three young children to care for?" Despite their sorrow, they would not budge but put their hope in God. After a difficult pregnancy, Maria delivered a healthy baby girl (their last child). They welcomed Enrichetta as a little miracle.

The Quattrocchis earnestly trained their children to seek the things above, joking that they wanted them to appreciate life "from the roof up." They trained themselves, too: "We studied books on child-rearing, seeking to improve ourselves and correct our faults for love of them," Maria wrote. They established a pattern of family prayer that centered around daily Mass and the evening rosary, to which neighbors were invited.

But they were hardly superspiritual. The family enjoyed sports and vacations. People dropped in and received a warm welcome. The atmosphere was serene "but not excessively pious," says Cesare (now Father Paolino). "I remember our house as noisily happy." This was especially the case at mealtimes, family friends recall.

The couple's love of God flowed out to others. Luigi, who rose to the position of Italy's assistant attorney general, did pro bono work and was a quiet, effective evangelist among colleagues and friends. Maria wrote numerous books on Christian marriage and family life. At fifty-two, she completed a nursing degree that qualified her for volunteer work with the Red Cross.

As a couple, the Quattrocchis took part in various projects, movements, and associations. They became Boy Scout supporters (the movement was just beginning in Italy), signed up their sons, and started a troop in a poor section of Rome.

Closer by, Maria and Luigi reached out to neighborhood families in need. They offered friendship, counsel, and religious instruction, along with material assistance. By opening their home to others, one person observed, the couple made it "a twenty-four hour a day health clinic for soul and body." During the German occupation of Rome, the couple took in numerous people who were in flight from the Nazis and did what they could to save Jewish families from being deported.

Despite the occasional flashes of drama, Maria and Luigi's married life was mostly ordinary looking from the outside. But the quiet heroism with which they met life's big and small challenges did not go unnoticed. Three decades after Maria's death in August 1965 (she survived Luigi by fourteen years), the official process for their canonization was begun.

A question arose at their beatification. Normally, a saint's feast day is assigned to the day of death—the day of birth into eternal life. If this practice were to be followed with Luigi and Maria, their feasts would fall on different days. But by special request of John Paul II, the Quattrocchis' will be celebrated as one on November 25—their wedding anniversary.

THE BLESSING OF CHILDREN

Questions to Begin

10 minutes
Use a question or two to get warmed up for the reading. Couples: try to guess your spouse's answers.

---

1 If you had to choose a name for a girl, what would it be? for a boy?

---

2 Identify a popular saying about child rearing that you have learned from experience is not always true.

---

3 When you were growing up, who did your parents want you *not* to hang around with?

May your children bring you happiness, and may your generous love for them be returned to you, many times over.

Wedding Mass, Final Blessing

Opening the Bible

10 minutes
Read the passage aloud. Let individuals take turns reading
paragraphs.

The Background

Here we read a couple of prayers from the Old Testament book of
Psalms. As prayers, they are written to be spoken to God; yet they
are addressed to parents—and carry an important message for
them. Then we dip into the book of Proverbs. Most of that biblical
book consists of short sayings, but the opening chapters contain
little lectures by parents to children. We read two of these. Our
excerpts focus on values, character, and relationships, which makes
them an excellent resource for self-examination by parents—and
the rest of us, too.

The Reading: Psalms 127 and 128; Proverbs 1:8–19; 3:13–31, 35

A Reminder about Depending on God

Psalm 127:1 Unless the LORD builds the house,
those who build it labor in vain.
Unless the LORD guards the city,
the guard keeps watch in vain.
2 It is in vain that you rise up early
and go late to rest,
eating the bread of anxious toil;
for he gives sleep to his beloved.

3 Sons are indeed a heritage from the LORD,
the fruit of the womb a reward.
4 Like arrows in the hand of a warrior
are the sons of one's youth.
5 Happy is the man who has
his quiver full of them.
He shall not be put to shame
when he speaks with his enemies in the gate.

17 For in vain is the net baited

A Promise of Blessings

Psalm 128:1 Happy is everyone who fears the LORD,
　　　　who walks in his ways.
2 You shall eat the fruit of the labor of your hands;
　　　　you shall be happy, and it shall go well with you.
3 Your wife will be like a fruitful vine
　　　　within your house;
　　your children will be like olive shoots
　　　　around your table.
4 Thus shall the man be blessed
　　　　who fears the LORD.

5 The LORD bless you from Zion.
　　　　May you see the prosperity of Jerusalem
　　　　all the days of your life.
6 May you see your children's children.
　　　　Peace be upon Israel!

A Parent Warns a Child

Proverbs 1:8 Hear, my child, your father's instruction,
　　　　and do not reject your mother's teaching;
9 for they are a fair garland for your head,
　　　　and pendants for your neck.

10 My child, if sinners entice you,
　　　　do not consent.
11 If they say, "Come with us, let us lie in wait for blood;
　　　　let us wantonly ambush the innocent. . . .
13 We shall find all kinds of costly things;
　　　　we shall fill our houses with booty.
14 Throw in your lot among us;
　　　　we will all have one purse"—
15 my child, do not walk in their way,
　　　　keep your foot from their paths;
16 for their feet run to evil,
　　　　and they hurry to shed blood.

while the bird is looking on;
¹⁸ yet they lie in wait—to kill themselves!
and set an ambush—for their own lives!
¹⁹ Such is the end of all who are greedy for gain;
it takes away the life of its possessors.

A Parent Speaks about Values

Proverbs 3:13 Happy are those who find wisdom,
and those who get understanding,
¹⁴ for her income is better than silver,
and her revenue better than gold.
¹⁵ She is more precious than jewels,
and nothing you desire can compare with her.
¹⁶ Long life is in her right hand;
in her left hand are riches and honor.
¹⁷ Her ways are ways of pleasantness,
and all her paths are peace.
¹⁸ She is a tree of life to those who lay hold of her;
those who hold her fast are called happy.

¹⁹ The LORD by wisdom founded the earth;
by understanding he established the heavens;
²⁰ by his knowledge the deeps broke open,
and the clouds drop down the dew.

²¹ My child, do not let these escape from your sight:
keep sound wisdom and prudence,
²² and they will be life for your soul
and adornment for your neck.
²³ Then you will walk on your way securely
and your foot will not stumble. . . .

²⁶ for the LORD will be your confidence
and will keep your foot from being caught.
²⁷ Do not withhold good from those to whom it is due,
when it is in your power to do it.

Exploring the Theme

28 Do not say to your neighbor, "Go, and come again, tomorrow I will give it"—when you have it with you.
29 Do not plan harm against your neighbor who lives trustingly beside you.
30 Do not quarrel with anyone without cause, when no harm has been done to you.
31 Do not envy the violent and do not choose any of their ways. . . .

35 The wise will inherit honor, but stubborn fools, disgrace.

First Impression

5 minutes
Briefly mention a question you have about the reading or one thing in it that surprised, impressed, delighted, or challenged you. No discussion! Just listen to one another's reactions.

4

If participants have not read this section already, read it aloud.
Otherwise go on to "Questions for Reflection and Discussion."

Psalms 127 and 128. Life can be frustrating. Sometimes work is "in vain" (127:1). We can achieve a lot with skill and effort; yet unpredictable factors may rob us of the results we expect. Farmers do not always "eat the fruit" of their "hands" (128:2). A farmer can toil for months, only to watch the crop be destroyed by an unexpected storm. In any case, the goal of our work often lies beyond our control. Building or buying a house? No problem, we can do that. What we cannot do is guarantee that our family will be healthy and happy once we move in.

So what do the psalmists recommend—sitting back and letting God do everything? That would be unrealistic and would fly in the face of what Scripture says about foresight and hard work (Proverbs 10:4–5). The psalmist is hardly suggesting that farmers sleep more and work less (127:2)—farm work is inescapably demanding. And guards who snoozed when they should be keeping watch would be worse than useless! Obviously, sleeping peacefully at night is better than lying awake, churning with anxiety; but there is work to be done in the morning.

The psalmists want us to remember that we are creatures, therefore limited in what we can achieve and dependent on God for the success of our efforts. The point of saying that children are a gift from the Lord (127:3) is not to convince us that it is good to have children but to remind us where they come from. The psalmists urge us to remember that God is the source of every good.

Being mindful of God is what the psalmists mean when they speak of fearing the Lord (128:1, 4). This fear means recognizing God as an awesome, present reality; it means living with an awareness that our lives are in his hands, that no good comes into existence except by his will, that our efforts will lead to happiness only if they are coordinated with his intentions. Such reverence for God is "the beginning of knowledge" (Proverbs 1:7).

St. Robert Bellarmine points out that "holy fear" of the Lord means walking "in his ways" (128:1), that is, in his commandments, and explains that "this holy fear proceeds from love." Consider Jesus' words, says Bellarmine: "They who have my commandments

59

and keep them are those who love me" (John 14:21). Reverence, obedience, love—relating to God this way is letting him build our house (Psalm 127:1).

Proverbs 1:8–19. The parent here (verse 8 implies that it could be father or mother) gives a child some straightforward advice: Don't join a gang. In some situations, then as now, this warning would be quite appropriate. Yet to many children, it might seem a little extreme. One can picture a fourteen-year-old looking up from his computer game and replying, "Chill out, Mom. My friends aren't dangerous criminals!" Yet Mom knows that children are naive. They underestimate dangers. The child tends to think, "Nothing really bad will happen to me." Having lived longer, Mom knows that the trip from a little experimentation with drugs to criminal activity to an early death can be terrifyingly shorter than the fourteen-year-old mind comprehends.

Many roads lie open to the young person. Each leads to a different destination, but the destinations are not easily apparent at the point of departure. Because of their life experience, parents are in a position to help children learn to scrutinize the signs at the entrance ramps in order to distinguish the dangerous allurements from the constructive opportunities (1:10).

That is what the parent is doing here. He or she points out that the big guys' swaggering offer to share their loot may be flattering and attractive to the youngster (1:14), but those who share these guys' takings will also share their fate. In their boasting, the gang members don't realize *whose* blood is going to be spilled (1:16)—and it won't just be their victims' blood. Sure, these guys *sound* like they can handle any problem; but, the parent cautions the child, they are actually dumber than birds. Birds have enough sense to stay out of a trap when they see it being laid; the gang members are so stupid that they will fall into the trap they themselves set (1:17–18).

Greed "takes away the life" of the greedy (1:19). Is the parent simplistically predicting that every single bad deed will have an equal and immediate painful effect? No, the mother or father is warning that a person's general behavior and character lead inevitably to happiness or unhappiness. The parent is well aware that people may for a time escape the consequences of their foolish actions. That is exactly why the parent is giving this warning. Afraid that the child will see the bad guys' short-term success and draw the wrong conclusion, the parent predicts that the gang members' foolish and evil ways of life will catch up with them sooner or later.

Proverbs 3:13–18. Parents naturally want their children to succeed. But more important than equipping children with the tools of success is helping them see what success *is*. The authors of the book of Proverbs view material prosperity as an aspect of success and talk about how to achieve it. But they insist that wealth by itself does not equal success. Success involves becoming wise, and true wisdom is oriented toward goals greater than material satisfactions. Wisdom leads to "riches and honor" (3:16)—an alternative translation would be "honorable riches"—and true wisdom shows us how to gain and use wealth in ways that our neighbors will honor because our actions benefit the community.

Proverbs 3:19–20. True wisdom consists of more than human insight; it contains a divine element (3:19–20). By his own wisdom, God created the magnificent universe. This divine wisdom has become visible in Jesus Christ, who is the Word, or wisdom, of God. God created all things "through him" (John 1:3). The essence of wise living, then, is to follow Jesus, to model ourselves on his humility and love. Training our children to do this is the heart of our responsibility as parents.

Proverbs 3:21–31, 35. The lecturing parent offers examples of wisdom in action.

♦ Verse 27: "Do not withhold good from those to whom it is due." More literally, the Hebrew says, "Do not withhold good from *its possessor.*" The assumption is that a person in need has a *claim* on needed resources, such a compelling claim, in fact, that he or she can be regarded as the rightful possessor of those resources!

♦ Verse 28 is not about charitable giving but about paying debts and returning what is borrowed or held in trust. Sometimes wisdom is just plain, uncomplicated integrity.

- Verse 29: "Do not plan harm against your neighbor who lives trustingly beside you"—or against anyone else, a rabbinical commentator adds.
- Verse 31. This puts the earlier lecture (Proverbs 1:8–19) in a nutshell. The parent warns the child not to admire evildoers who seem to get ahead.

Reflections. Our psalms lead to a practical conclusion. If God blesses those who revere him, and if revering him involves obeying him, then those of us who are parents should get sin, especially serious sin, out of our lives, in order to experience God's blessing on our families.

But these psalms not only warn us; they also encourage us. In dealing with children, much lies beyond our control. We cannot make a crying newborn go to sleep or make an adult child return to faith in God. Yet, the psalmists reassure us, there is no need to throw up our hands in despair in the face of difficulties, for there is no limit to what God can do. Our children are a blessing from God—and he is capable of blessing them with whatever guidance and grace they need at every stage of life. The psalmists invite us to imitate the farmer who works hard during the day but sleeps soundly at night, knowing that the results are in God's hands (Mark 4:26–27).

Our readings from Proverbs highlight the process of passing on the fruit of our life experience to our children. Imparting character and values is of utmost importance here, far outweighing the importance of teaching particular skills or information.

It is a little scary to realize that we *do* inevitably communicate our values and mold our children's character, for good or ill, simply by living with them year after year. Our children are exposed to our immaturity as well as to our maturity. Yet, perfection is not required of parents. What *is* required is our making progress on the road of wisdom along which we hope to lead our children. We must do what we can and rely on God to do what we cannot. Isn't that the message of Psalms 127 and 128?

Questions for Reflection and Discussion

45 minutes
Choose questions according to your interest and time.

Questions for All

1   Psalm 127:3–5 is directed to a husband. What equivalent statement might be made to a wife?

2   Psalm 128:3–4 is also directed to the husband. Again, what might the equivalent statement to the wife contain? Try saying it in a psalmlike style.

3   What are some ways that children are a blessing to their parents?

4   Proverbs 3:17 expresses a parent's view. Would a child always see things this way? When might a parent have a hard time getting a child to accept the view of wisdom stated in this verse?

5   Give an example of a parent's strength of character rubbing off on a child. Without trashing anyone, can you give an example of a parent's character defects affecting a child? Do children follow what they see their parents doing, regardless of what their parents say? When have you seen exceptions— positive and negative—to this pattern?

Questions for Spouses

If you don't have children yet, consider how these questions apply to you as possible future parents.

6 What do you feel is your greatest need as a parent at the present time? Where could you get help in meeting it?

7 What attitudes and approaches to money and material things are your children picking up from you? What do your words and deeds say to them about the importance of using one's resources in service of other people?

8 For personal reflection: How can a parent get an objective reading on his or her strengths and weaknesses and on the impact they are having on the children? Who might help you as a parent make this kind of self-assessment?

9 **Focus question.** Pick one of the topics that has come up in the reading or discussion, and talk about it as a couple. Suggested starter questions for considering your topic: Where do we stand? What are our strong points? What do we need to change? How can we support each other? What help do we need to get? How will we entrust this to God's care?

Prayer to Close

10 minutes
Use one of these approaches—or create your own!

♦ For families you know—or for your own family or family of origin—pray together a psalm of thanksgiving (suggestions: Psalms 34 or 100), repentance (Psalms 25 or 51), appeal for help (Psalms 77 or 123), or trust in God (Psalms 23, 57, or 91). End with an Our Father.

♦ Spouses: Spend a few moments expressing aloud your needs as parents and offering yourselves to God to be his agents for good in your home. Close by praying Psalm 127 or 128 together.

At Work in the World

Questions to Begin

10 minutes
Use a question or two to get warmed up for the reading. Couples: try to guess your spouse's answers.

1 Have you ever been taken in by a sales pitch or marketing ploy?

2 If you could choose a gift or ability, what would it be?

May you always bear witness to the love of God in this world
so that the afflicted and the needy
will find in you generous friends
and welcome you into the joys of heaven.

Wedding Mass, Final Blessing

Opening the Bible

10 minutes
Read the passage aloud. Let individuals take turns reading paragraphs. Suggestion for couples: read the passage from the Gospel of John twice, the second time substituting your own names for "they" and "them."

The Background

St. Paul spoke of marriage as an image of Christ's love for the Church (Ephesians 5—Week 1). On this basis, Christian tradition has recognized the family as a microcosm of the Church. As minichurch, the family has not only an inward reality but also an outward one: Christ is present in the family not only for the married couple and their children but also for people outside the family circle. The married couple, with their children, are called to be an expression of Christ's love in the world. With this in mind, we read three excerpts from the New Testament on the mission of the Church. None of the excerpts speaks explicitly about marriage, but all of them have important implications for Christian marriage.

In our first reading, Jesus is praying for his disciples as they sit at table with him at the Last Supper—and for us, his later followers (John 17:20). Jesus is about to go out and meet those who will arrest him and have him put to death. His prayer concludes and sums up his work on earth. As the prayer shows, he came into the world to make God known, to create a new, deeper, more intimate bond between God his Father and his human brothers and sisters. Jesus prays that we would be united in his love as he sends us out to continue his mission in the world.

In our second reading, Jesus gives some definition to the mission on which he sends us: to show compassion for the afflicted.

Our third reading, from St. Paul's letter to the Ephesians, speaks of the gifts of the Spirit, which empower us to carry out our mission.

The Reading: John 17:17–26; Matthew 25:31–40; Ephesians 4:4–7, 11–16

Jesus Speaks to His Father on Behalf of His Followers

John 17:17 "Sanctify them in the truth; your word is truth. 18 As you have sent me into the world, so I have sent them into the world.

67

19 And for their sakes I sanctify myself, so that they also may be sanctified in truth.

20 "I ask not only on behalf of these, but also on behalf of those who will believe in me through their word, 21 that they may all be one. As you, Father, are in me and I am in you, may they also be in us, so that the world may believe that you have sent me. 22 The glory that you have given me I have given them, so that they may be one, as we are one, 23 I in them and you in me, that they may become completely one, so that the world may know that you have sent me and have loved them even as you have loved me. 24 Father, I desire that those also, whom you have given me, may be with me where I am, to see my glory, which you have given me because you loved me before the foundation of the world.

25 "Righteous Father, the world does not know you, but I know you; and these know that you have sent me. 26 I made your name known to them, and I will make it known, so that the love with which you have loved me may be in them, and I in them."

The Service Jesus Seeks

Matthew 25:31 "When the Son of Man comes in his glory, and all the angels with him, then he will sit on the throne of his glory. 32 All the nations will be gathered before him, and he will separate people one from another as a shepherd separates the sheep from the goats, 33 and he will put the sheep at his right hand and the goats at the left. 34 Then the king will say to those at his right hand, 'Come, you that are blessed by my Father, inherit the kingdom prepared for you from the foundation of the world; 35 for I was hungry and you gave me food, I was thirsty and you gave me something to drink, I was a stranger and you welcomed me, 36 I was naked and you gave me clothing, I was sick and you took care of me, I was in prison and you visited me.' 37 Then the righteous will answer him, 'Lord, when was it that we saw you hungry and gave you food, or thirsty and gave you something to drink? 38 And when was it that we saw you a stranger and welcomed you, or naked and gave you clothing? 39 And when was it that we saw you sick or in prison and visited you?' 40 And the king will answer them, 'Truly I tell you, just as you did it to one of the least of these who are members of my family,* you did it to me.'"

The Empowerment Jesus Gives

Ephesians 4:4 There is one body and one Spirit, just as you were called to the one hope of your calling, 5 one Lord, one faith, one baptism, 6 one God and Father of all, who is above all and through all and in all.

7 But each of us was given grace according to the measure of Christ's gift. . . . 11 The gifts he gave were that some would be apostles, some prophets, some evangelists, some pastors and teachers, 12 to equip the saints for the work of ministry, for building up the body of Christ, 13 until all of us come to the unity of the faith and of the knowledge of the Son of God, to maturity, to the measure of the full stature of Christ. 14 We must no longer be children, tossed to and fro and blown about by every wind of doctrine, by people's trickery, by their craftiness in deceitful scheming. 15 But speaking the truth in love, we must grow up in every way into him who is the head, into Christ, 16 from whom the whole body, joined and knit together by every ligament with which it is equipped, as each part is working properly, promotes the body's growth in building itself up in love.

*Greek *these my brothers*

First Impression

5 minutes
Briefly mention a question you have about the reading or one thing in it that surprised, impressed, delighted, or challenged you. No discussion! Just listen to one another's reactions.

Exploring the Theme

If participants have not read this section already, read it aloud. Otherwise go on to "Questions for Reflection and Discussion."

John 17:17–26. Jesus' prayer that we be made one in him embraces not only the Church as a whole but every family. His desire is for every husband and wife to be united with him and with one another.

Jesus unites us with himself in order to send us, on his behalf, to others. He says to his Father, "As you have sent me into the world, so I have sent them into the world" (17:18). He intends to continue to reveal God's love to men and women through us. This is his call to the Church as a whole and to every Jon and Mari, every Mike and Midge.

As Jesus' prayer makes plain, our part in his work begins with being united with him and with one another. The spouses' unity with each other is part of what they offer to the world (17:23). "See," they can say, "Christ's love is so real it enables *us* to live together and grow in love!" There is truth in the familiar saying that the best thing a father can do for his children is to love their mother. It is also true that the best thing a husband and wife can do for the Church and the world is to fulfill their calling to be united with each other in Christ's love.

Married couples struggle with differences of viewpoint, priorities, and approach—not to mention each other's failings and sins. Jesus' prayer reminds us that the source of unity for each couple, as for the whole Church, is God himself. Unity is a gift of God, which is why Jesus petitions the Father to give it to us (17:20–21). Of course, unity is also a challenge for spouses, a task that is sometimes arduous and daunting; yet it remains basically a gift of God, something found in him. Unity comes only as husband and wife strive for it; yet their striving for it is the way of receiving what God wishes to give.

"I in them," Jesus says of his relationship with his followers (17:23). Here is the starting point for every married couple's service in the world.

Matthew 25:31–40. On the implications of Jesus' words, John Paul II offers this reflection:

Fathers and mothers, sons and daughters, will be judged by their actions. . . . Christ will be the judge. . . . His will be a *judgment on love*. . . . "Come, O blessed of my Father . . . for I was hungry and you gave me food, I was thirsty and you gave me drink. . . ." This list could of course be lengthened, and countless other problems relevant to married and family life could be added. There we might very well find statements like: "I was an unborn child, and you welcomed me by letting me be born"; "I was an abandoned child, and you became my family"; "I was an orphan, and you adopted me and raised me as one of your own children." Or again: "You helped mothers filled with uncertainty and exposed to wrongful pressure to welcome their unborn child and let it be born," and "You helped large families and families in difficulty to look after and educate the children God gave them." . . . This is *the great harvest* which the Redeemer of the world . . . will come to reap.

Ephesians 4:4–7, 11–16. Where can ordinary people, including married couples, find the motivation and power to participate in Christ's mission? St. Paul's answer is simple: the Lord gives us graces, capacities, talents—"gifts" (4:11). The gifts Paul mentions here seem rather exalted. "Some" are apostles, Paul says. We can nod our heads and agree that *some* are—and most of us aren't! But Paul does not mean his list of spiritual gifts to be comprehensive (for another sampling, see 1 Corinthians 12). God gives many kinds of gifts. Individuals and couples have the challenge of discovering them, developing them, and putting them to use for the good of other people.

Paul envisions the Christian community growing to maturity through members using their gifts for one another (4:15–16). It is crucial for "each part" to function properly (4:16). Long experience demonstrates that the local Christian community, the parish, gets "knit together" in love only when families get involved and become the ligaments, the connecting tissue, of the body (see 4:16). For many families, the parish is the main framework for developing their gifts of service. But there is a world of needs and a myriad of ways in which couples and families can serve. Whatever the direction of your gifts, and no matter how humble they may be, what counts is to use them to complete the work that God gives you.

Reflections. A tension runs through the Christian vision of marriage. On the one hand, spouses need to create a home and make it a pleasant place for themselves and their children. Often, they must struggle to do this in the face of resistance: a thousand demands and attractions blur their focus on making a home; financially, homemaking is often a great strain. On the other hand, if spouses focus their time, attention, and money on making a pleasant home while neglecting the rest of the world, their marriage will be stunted in terms of Christ's call—and they will pass on a distorted set of values to their children. Both the inward and outward callings are built into Christian marriage.

The Christian family is designed for more than itself. Thus, Christian leaders have traditionally urged families to devote themselves to social service, to practice hospitality in all its forms, and to be politically active on behalf of laws that support and defend the rights of the family, children, and the needy.

In the fourth century, St. John Chrysostom urged Christian couples to invite not only family and friends to their wedding but also Christ. "Do you know how to invite him?" John asked. "'Whatsoever you do to the least of my brothers,' he said, 'you do to me.' So don't think that it is annoying to invite the poor for Christ's sake." For any brides and grooms not persuaded by this startling advice, John had a comeback. "No one in the city has done this, you say? Why don't you hurry to be the founder of this good custom, so that posterity may attribute it to you?" John's words challenge each couple to think about how their family life can be of service to the needy—and how to be open to new and unexpected ways of putting their gifts to work.

Questions for Reflection and Discussion

45 minutes
Choose questions according to your interest and time.

Questions for All

1 How might any part of Jesus' prayer in John 17 be reworded and enlarged to be prayed by parents—and other adults—for children?

2 In what personal relationship could you act this week to restore or develop unity?

3 If you were to further enlarge Jesus' list in Matthew 25:31–40 à la John Paul II (see page 71), who would you add? What could you do for those you add?

4 How might Ephesians 4:15 apply to marriage? Illustrate your view with examples.

Questions for Spouses

5 What priority do you place on unity in your marriage? Does unity in marriage mean having the same opinion about every issue? What approaches to decision making foster unity—or division—between spouses?

6 Paul speaks of evangelists and pastors (Ephesians 4:11). In what ways do parents serve as evangelists and pastors for their children?

7 Paul also speaks of teaching as a spiritual gift (Ephesians 4:11). How does the help of the Holy Spirit enter into teaching a child how to receive Holy Communion? how to roast a turkey? how to fish for walleye? how to drive a car? how to tell the truth? how to deal with bullies? Do you pray for the gifts and graces you need as a parent?

8 **Focus question.** What are your gifts as individuals? as a couple? as a family? Through what experiences have the gifts God has given you and the mission he has called you to as a couple become clearer to you over the course of your marriage? How could you encourage and support one another in using your gifts for others? Are there ways that you discourage each other from using your gifts? Do you support each other or compete with each other in using your gifts?

Prayer to Close

10 minutes
Use this approach—or create your own!

♦ Pray this prayer together. End with a Hail Mary and an Our Father.

Lord, share your heart with us. Make us of one heart with you. Only in this way can we be of one heart with each other. Give us your love for the people around us, and guide us in using our resources and talents on their behalf. Help us to let go of our comforts and securities and launch out with you into the work you have for us in the world.

Saints in the Making

Prisca and Aquila: St. Paul's Employers, Colleagues, and Friends

This section is a supplement for individual reading.

It was in the great commercial city of Corinth that Paul first showed up on Prisca and Aquila's doorstep (Acts 18:2). The couple had relocated to Corinth following the expulsion of Jews from Rome in AD 49. Paul, who was on a missionary journey, was there to preach the gospel. He was probably searching out employment opportunities rather than converts when he stopped by to see the pair, however. Aquila and Prisca were already baptized Christians, it seems (Scripture makes no mention of Paul's evangelizing them), and they ran a family business, making leather and canvas tents and awnings. Paul, also a "tentmaker," found not just work but lodging and friendship with them (Acts 18:3).

Prisca and Aquila, in turn, joined in Paul's apostolic work. One imagines their collaboration evolving as they cut and stitched in the workshop together, discussing the good news of Jesus and, undoubtedly, sharing it with anyone who dropped in. When the apostle moved on to Ephesus a year and a half later, the couple pulled up stakes and went with him (Acts 18:11, 18). Their trade facilitated mobility: tentmakers were in demand everywhere, and they could travel light, their only tools a knife, awl, needles, and thread.

The family business must have yielded a decent living— enough for Aquila and Prisca to practice generous hospitality, as well as support themselves and any children they may have had. Both in Ephesus and in Rome, where they later returned, they owned houses large enough to host church gatherings (1 Corinthians 16:19; Romans 16:3–5).

A picture emerges of a talented, initiative-taking couple who worked well together and were alert to evangelistic opportunities. When they heard an eloquent but only partially catechized speaker named Apollos preaching about Jesus in a synagogue, Prisca and Aquila took him home. Without offending him or being cowed by his intelligence, they gave him the instruction he lacked (Acts 18:24–28).

Sometimes the intrepid couple took greater chances. They "risked their necks for my life," Paul wrote, without supplying details (Romans 16:4). Perhaps they used their influence to intervene on his behalf when his preaching occasioned attacks and even a riot (read Acts 18:12–17 and 19:23–41, and use your imagination!). No wonder the apostle trusted them as friends and fellow missionaries "who work with me in Christ Jesus" (Romans 16:3)—a wonderful example for clergy and laypeople to ponder today.

Unlike Paul, Prisca and Aquila were not always free to hit the road; but wherever they were, they used their time, resources, and opportunities to build up the Church. And by making their home a place of welcome, they met needs that a traveling apostle could not.

The couple's example of hospitality calls us on. Admittedly, their social situation was different from ours. In the ancient world, businesspeople like Prisca and Aquila lived with extended family and others in households where many activities took place: raising and teaching children, producing and selling goods, and caring for the sick and the elderly. Because much of this activity happens outside the modern household, we may have fewer at-home opportunities to receive others in Jesus' name. Even so, we are held to the same ideal: "I was a stranger and you welcomed me" (Matthew 25:35).

A blessing in the wedding Mass urges couples to "always bear witness to the love of God in this world so that the afflicted and the needy will find in you generous friends." With Prisca and Aquila in mind, couples might sit down together and do some assessing: *Are we living this out? Are there people we should be bringing into the family circle? Do we show Christ's love to those who enter our home? How can we teach our children to be hospitable?* Husbands and wives might ask Aquila and Prisca to intercede for them as they ponder these questions.

Prisca and Aquila put their mobility at the service of the gospel. So can all of us. Whenever we travel, we can seek opportunities to bring Christ to others. Every day, we cross paths with people who will never cross our thresholds. But with a mentality of "mobile hospitality," we and our children can welcome the people we encounter in our parish, school, workplace, neighborhood, and city. Additionally, we can find ways of visiting prisoners, the housebound, and other "strangers" in special need.

Paul gratefully acknowledged the work of Prisca and Aquila, "to whom not only I give thanks, but also all the churches of the Gentiles" (Romans 16:4). For their perennial example of missionary dedication in marriage, we can give thanks, too.

At Cana, Always

Questions to Begin

10 minutes
Use a question or two to get warmed up for the reading. Couples: try to guess your spouse's answers.

1 At the end of a social event, I:
❑ like to leave right away;
❑ don't mind hanging around for a while and talking with people;
❑ somehow always end up being the last to leave.

2 When you have to remember something, what aids do you use?

May the Lord Jesus, who was a guest at the wedding in Cana,
bless you and your families and friends.
May Jesus, who loved his Church to the end,
always fill your hearts with his love.
May he grant that, as you believe in his resurrection,
so you may wait for him in joy and hope.

Wedding Mass, Final Blessing

Opening the Bible

6 *Selections from John 2 and 14–15*

10 minutes
Read the passage aloud. Let individuals take turns reading paragraphs.

The Background

Our Scripture readings have helped us consider various aspects of marriage—lovemaking and child rearing, good times and hard times, serving neighbors. Christ makes himself present in all these aspects of married life. We end our reflections here thinking not about any of the aspects of marriage where Christ makes himself present, but about Christ himself, and about his being present with married couples—and with us all—by his Holy Spirit.

Our readings contain two episodes from the Gospel of John. In the first, Jesus, on the brink of launching out into his public ministry, relaxes with family and friends at a wedding reception. In the second episode (our second and third readings), his ministry has come to an end, and he is sharing his final meal with his closest friends before going out to meet those who will arrest him and have him put to death.

The Reading: John 2:1–11; 14:15–29; 15:1–17

Jesus Brings Joy to a Wedding

John 2:1 . . . [T]here was a wedding in Cana of Galilee, and the mother of Jesus was there. 2 Jesus and his disciples had also been invited to the wedding. 3 When the wine gave out, the mother of Jesus said to him, "They have no wine." 4 And Jesus said to her, "Woman, what concern is that to you and to me? My hour has not yet come." 5 His mother said to the servants, "Do whatever he tells you."

6 Now standing there were six stone water jars for the Jewish rites of purification, each holding twenty or thirty gallons. 7 Jesus said to them, "Fill the jars with water." And they filled them up to the brim. 8 He said to them, "Now draw some out, and take it to the chief steward." So they took it.

9 When the steward tasted the water that had become wine, and did not know where it came from (though the servants who had drawn the water knew), the steward called the bridegroom 10 and said to him, "Everyone serves the good wine first, and then the

inferior wine after the guests have become drunk. But you have kept the good wine until now."

11 Jesus did this, the first of his signs, in Cana of Galilee, and revealed his glory; and his disciples believed in him.

Jesus Promises to Dwell in His Followers

14:15 "If you love me, you will keep my commandments. 16 And I will ask the Father, and he will give you another Advocate, to be with you forever. 17 This is the Spirit of truth, whom the world cannot receive, because it neither sees him nor knows him. You know him, because he abides with you, and he will be in you.

18 "I will not leave you orphaned; I am coming to you. 19 In a little while the world will no longer see me, but you will see me; because I live, you also will live. 20 On that day you will know that I am in my Father, and you in me, and I in you. 21 They who have my commandments and keep them are those who love me; and those who love me will be loved by my Father, and I will love them and reveal myself to them."

22 Judas (not Iscariot) said to him, "Lord, how is it that you will reveal yourself to us, and not to the world?"

23 Jesus answered him, "Those who love me will keep my word, and my Father will love them, and we will come to them and make our home with them. 24 Whoever does not love me does not keep my words; and the word that you hear is not mine, but is from the Father who sent me.

25 "I have said these things to you while I am still with you. 26 But the Advocate, the Holy Spirit, whom the Father will send in my name, will teach you everything, and remind you of all that I have said to you. 27 Peace I leave with you; my peace I give to you. I do not give to you as the world gives. Do not let your hearts be troubled, and do not let them be afraid. 28 You heard me say to you, 'I am going away, and I am coming to you.' If you loved me, you would rejoice that I am going to the Father, because the Father is greater than I. 29 And now I have told you this before it occurs, so that when it does occur, you may believe. . . ."

Jesus Calls His Followers to Abide in Him

15:1 "I am the true vine, and my Father is the vinegrower. 2 He removes every branch in me that bears no fruit. Every branch that bears fruit he prunes to make it bear more fruit. 3 You have already been cleansed by the word that I have spoken to you. 4 Abide in me as I abide in you. Just as the branch cannot bear fruit by itself unless it abides in the vine, neither can you unless you abide in me. 5 I am the vine, you are the branches. Those who abide in me and I in them bear much fruit, because apart from me you can do nothing. 6 Whoever does not abide in me is thrown away like a branch and withers; such branches are gathered, thrown into the fire, and burned. 7 If you abide in me, and my words abide in you, ask for whatever you wish, and it will be done for you. 8 My Father is glorified by this, that you bear much fruit and become my disciples. 9 As the Father has loved me, so I have loved you; abide in my love. 10 If you keep my commandments, you will abide in my love, just as I have kept my Father's commandments and abide in his love. 11 I have said these things to you so that my joy may be in you, and that your joy may be complete.

12 "This is my commandment, that you love one another as I have loved you. 13 No one has greater love than this, to lay down one's life for one's friends. 14 You are my friends if you do what I command you. 15 I do not call you servants any longer, because the servant does not know what the master is doing; but I have called you friends, because I have made known to you everything that I have heard from my Father. 16 You did not choose me but I chose you. And I appointed you to go and bear fruit, fruit that will last, so that the Father will give you whatever you ask him in my name. 17 I am giving you these commands so that you may love one another."

First Impression

5 minutes
Briefly mention a question you have about the reading or one thing in it that surprised, impressed, delighted, or challenged you. No discussion! Just listen to one another's reactions.

Exploring the Theme

If participants have not read this section already, read it aloud. Otherwise go on to "Questions for Reflection and Discussion."

2:1–11. In first-century Galilee, wedding celebrations lasted for days. Running out of wine may not have been unusual. Probably, however, the wine would run out only after the party had been going for a while. Thus, it seems that Jesus was in no hurry to leave. Presumably he was enjoying himself. Since the bride and groom were family friends, he may have known them since childhood. He was about to begin his public ministry (2:12). From this point on, he would travel from village to village, with only an occasional visit to his hometown, Nazareth. Attending the wedding celebration in Cana marked the end of his living a settled life in Galilee. Did a touch of nostalgia make him reluctant to leave the party? In any case, his presence there made a statement to the newlyweds: "It's wonderful that you're married!"

Changing the water into wine was the first sign by which Jesus indicated the nature of his mission. The water jars, used for Jewish ritual cleansing, symbolized God's covenant through Moses. The wine's presence in the jars symbolizes the new age, the new relationship with God that Jesus will now bring. The wine's purpose—to keep the wedding celebration going—hints at the happiness of the new era. And through the miracle, Jesus says something not only about his mission but also about marriage. Quite simply, he endorses it.

The "whatever" (2:5) in Mary's instruction to the servants suggests that she did not know what her son would do. But the word also shows her trust in him—her conviction that anything he might do would deserve everyone's full cooperation. Spurred by his mother, Jesus provided for the couple's first need in their life together. His action stands as a lasting reminder to every couple that he is ready to help when needs arise.

By changing water into wine, Jesus took something naturally good and made it into something better. This is a clue to his intentions for marriage. He wishes to transform the great natural gift of marriage into something better—into a foretaste of the heavenly kingdom by leading husband and wife to love one another in a way that only he can make possible. Couples who stick with the process and arrive in old age together often testify that, as at Cana, the best wine is saved until last.

14:15–29. Jesus was present in Cana as the bride and groom began their marriage. But he could not continue to be physically in their home while carrying out his mission in the world. This is the kind of limitation he has in mind when he tells his disciples now, at the Last Supper, "It is to your advantage that I go away, for if I do not go away, the Advocate will not come to you"—the "Advocate" being the Holy Spirit (John 16:7). When Jesus departs physically, the Spirit comes. Through the Spirit, Jesus will dwell in all his followers in all their homes, from Cana to Kansas City. He will be with spouses not only at their wedding but to the end of their lives.

The Holy Spirit, Jesus tells us, will make God's love known to us; he will comfort, empower, and instruct us (14:18, 21, 26–27). These are promises of an experiential relationship with God. Wives and husbands are invited to enter into the experience as a couple. How? Jesus tells us that having faith in him and loving him by keeping his word are essential conditions for receiving the Spirit (14:15, 21, 23).

John Paul II describes the Holy Spirit as the living gift of God's love for spouses. "The gift of the Spirit is," he writes, "a stimulating impulse so that every day they may progress towards an ever richer union with each other on all levels—of the body, of the character, of the heart, of the intelligence and will, of the soul." The Spirit takes the command to love and "engraves it more profoundly on the hearts of Christian husbands and wives." By Jesus' action, marriage, like the water jars at Cana, becomes filled with something new.

15:1–17. Having spoken about his living in us by his Spirit, Jesus turns things around and speaks of our living in him. He promises that as he lives in us and we live in him, we will experience his joy. This joy, symbolized by the wine at Cana, will be made real by his presence.

Jesus encourages us to pray for our needs (15:7, 16). This is not a matter of shouting up at the sky. Through the Spirit, the Father comes to us, and Jesus comes to us (14:21, 23). The God to whom we make our needs known is not distant; he lives within us. He is intimately involved in every detail of our lives.

Jesus' call to abide in him is a spur to married couples to consider the place of prayer in their life together. Three forms of prayer are especially important.

The Mass. Jesus declares that "No one has greater love than this, to lay down one's life for one's friends" (15:13). Jesus' greatest-of-all love, expressed in his laying down of his life for us, becomes present to us in the Mass. Thus, the Mass is the natural center of spouses' prayers. The eucharistic sacrifice, John Paul II points out, "represents Christ's covenant of love with the Church, sealed with His blood on the Cross. In this sacrifice of the New and Eternal Covenant, Christian spouses encounter the source from which their own marriage covenant flows. . . . In the Eucharistic gift of charity the Christian family finds the foundation and soul of its 'communion' and its 'mission.'"

Family prayer. This takes many forms. In addition to regular times of prayer, the experiences of ordinary life present opportunities for spontaneously asking God for help and thanking him for blessings. In whatever way a family prays, it is wise to make a place for Mary, whose intercession for a bride and groom played such an important part at Cana and serves as an example of trust in her son. Many families make the rosary their main family prayer.

Prayer as a couple. This, too, of course, takes many forms. As with every form of prayer, even a little on a regular basis is invaluable.

Reflections. Artists have painted many depictions of the miracle at Cana. One might ask which depiction is the best. We suggest that the best representation of the miracle at Cana is a husband and wife whom Christ transforms (more slowly than the water at Cana!) into a visible image of his presence for each other, for their children, and for others.

Friends of ours who were married many years ago say that they have always been guided by a statement the priest made in his homily at their wedding: "One thing you have to remember: Cana is forever." That is a reminder to us all.

Questions for Reflection and Discussion

45 minutes
Choose questions according to your interest and time.

Questions for All

1 In John 2:9–10, were the groom and the steward aware that the wine had run out?

2 Why *do* people serve the better wine first (2:10)?

3 In what way is Mary at Cana a model for married couples? for every follower of Jesus?

4 When have you experienced the presence of the Holy Spirit? What can people do to open themselves to him?

5 What significance does Jesus' promise in John 14:27 have for you as a present or future parent, godparent, or friend of young people?

Questions for Spouses

6 What kinds of things can a couple do to participate in the Mass together?

7 What signs of God's presence in your marriage and family seem remarkable to you, even if people outside the family wouldn't appreciate their significance?

8   How do you mark Sunday as the Lord's Day as a couple? as a family? (See *Catechism of the Catholic Church*, section 1166–67.)

9   For personal reflection: Where does your marriage most need the Holy Spirit? What will you do to pray for his coming?

10   **Focus question.** What does it mean to have a relationship with Christ *as a couple*? What kind of relationship do you have with him as a couple? What would bring the two of you closer to him?

10 minutes
Use this approach—or create your own!

♦ Pray together this prayer for
  married couples, adapted
  from the nuptial blessing in
  the wedding liturgy. (Couples:
  pray for yourselves by changing
  "they" to "we," and so on.)

  Father, to reveal the plan of your
        love,
  you made the union of husband
        and wife
  an image of the covenant
        between you and your
        people.
  Lord, grant that as they live this
        sacrament
  they may share with each other
        the gifts of your love
  and become one in heart and
        mind
  as witnesses to your presence in
        their marriage.
  Help them to maintain a home
        together
  and give them the blessings they
        need
  to be good and faithful to one
        another.
  Father, grant that as they come
        together to your table on
        earth
  they may one day have the joy of
        sharing together
  your feast in heaven.

The Holy Couple

Joseph and Mary of Nazareth didn't have to look far to find Christ in their marriage. From the beginning of their life together, he was right there, in the flesh. But did the Holy Couple live out their unique calling within a real marriage? Was their house a home where a husband and wife drew close through the ups and downs of family life, or was it more like a monastery? Some early Church writers waffled on these questions. They were fighting heresies that attacked the belief that Mary remained a virgin throughout her life and that Jesus was God's Son—not the best time to draw attention to the Holy Couple's relationship. But with these few early exceptions, Church tradition has not hesitated to hail Mary and Joseph as the married couple par excellence, the husband and wife who best reveal the beauty of human love and the majesty of God's plan for marriage.

Granted, the couple's marriage and family life were unique. Yet Joseph and Mary were real spouses, real parents. Even though Joseph was not biologically Jesus' father, he was father to him in every other human way. And Joseph and Mary stood in the closest possible relationship to the Incarnation, the mystery of God with us in the everyday. In union with their Son, they are models and intercessors for all who seek to grow in understanding of Christian marriage. We can view them in terms of the six themes we have considered in this guide.

To Love and to Honor. As indicated by the creation accounts in Genesis 1 and 2, every marriage begins a wondrous new world. This is especially true of Joseph and Mary, who were called by God to receive and nurture a Son who would make "all things new" (Revelation 21:5). In two separate annunciations—one to Mary, another to Joseph (Luke 1:26–38; Matthew 1:20–23)— each is invited to advance the hidden plan of the Incarnation. Their yes, expressed separately but lived out as husband and wife, inaugurates a new creation.

"At the beginning of the New Testament, as at the beginning of the Old, there is a married couple," Pope Paul VI commented. "But whereas Adam and Eve were the source of evil which was unleashed on the world, Joseph and Mary are the summit from which holiness spreads all over the earth." Their union begins the work of salvation, revealing God's intent to sanctify the family as a "sanctuary of love and cradle of life."

Every Christian couple is meant to be a special reflection and channel of God's love for the human race. In the Holy Couple, this goal was dramatically realized.

To Have and to Hold. Most of us would shrink from the thought of reading the Song of Songs with the Holy Couple in mind. John Paul II does not. They "renewed the experience of 'fairest love' described in the Song of Solomon," he says. "Joseph thinks of Mary in the words: 'My sister, my bride' (Song 4:9). Mary, the mother of God, conceives by the power of the Holy Spirit, who is the origin of the 'fairest love.'"

John Paul II is not implying that Joseph and Mary had a sexual relationship. But putting the Song of Songs on their lips highlights the fact that they were a man and a woman in love, who saw one another's beauty, were drawn by it, and made a total gift of self for the other's good. Joseph expressed his generous, self-sacrificing love by taking Mary into his house, while respecting the fact that she belonged exclusively to God. Mary surrendered herself to Joseph's care, in accordance with God's plan.

John Paul II observes: "Joseph, in obedience to the Spirit, found in the Spirit the source of love, the conjugal love which he experienced as a man. And this love proved to be greater than this 'just man' could ever have expected within the limits of his human heart." Might we not suppose that, in her marriage to Joseph, Mary's love as a woman was also given new birth by the Spirit?

For Better, for Worse. Simeon's prophecy, the flight to Egypt, the massacre of the Bethlehem boys, finding Jesus in the temple—the Holy Couple must have wondered about the divine purpose behind these sufferings and hardships. Though they had some knowledge of God's saving plan and their part in it, they didn't have the whole picture. Like every Christian couple saying, "I do," they were on a pilgrimage of faith.

Joseph's pilgrimage was shorter than Mary's. (Since he never appears after the temple episode, the logical conclusion is that he died before Jesus began his public ministry.) Mary journeyed on to face the great test of faith at Jesus' crucifixion, which seemed to negate everything God had promised at the Annunciation. But while they were together, Mary and Joseph pondered, responded, and helped one another toward the hope that was set before them. "My mother and my brothers are those who hear the word of God and do it," Jesus once said (Luke 8:21). By this definition, too, Mary is Jesus' mother. Throughout her life, her faith revealed her as the model disciple. Blessed is she who believed that what the Lord spoke to her would be fulfilled (Luke 1:45)!

Likewise, Joseph, who so readily obeyed God's word received in dreams (Matthew 1:24; 2:14, 21), was a man of faith. His yes, expressed not in word but in obedient action, marks him out as the perfect match for the woman who said "let it be with me according to your word" (Luke 1:38).

The Blessing of Children. In Jesus' day, a child's first teacher was probably his mother, with both parents setting an example of prayer and religious observance. As a boy grew beyond infancy—after his third birthday, some scholars think—his father assumed the main responsibility for his religious training.

Did Mary and Joseph feel equipped for the task of teaching Jesus, divine wisdom made visible? Were they abashed after finding him in discussion with the temple scholars? However they felt, they rose to the challenge of raising and forming God's only Son. Quite simply, they trusted that God, who had called them to their unique task, would supply the gifts to carry it out.

Who is equal to the tasks of raising and teaching children, every couple wonders. "We don't have the patience, the love, the wisdom. . . ." But there is hope for every parent. If we put our faith in God, he will equip us to love and teach the children he has sent us.

At Work in the World. With their entire selves, the Holy Couple served the body of Christ in a very literal way. By fulfilling their calling to be united with one another in God's love in their marriage, they advanced God's plan of love for the human race. From the home they made, the Word of God went out to speak salvation to all.

Joseph and Mary undoubtedly did the works of mercy that their son would later identify as indispensable to entering the kingdom of God (Matthew 25:31–40). But their loving obedience to a plan they did not fully grasp was the greatest mercy of all.

How did they experience their calling? The Magnificat may provide a clue. Though the prayer was spoken by Mary when she visited Elizabeth (Luke 1:46–55), we can imagine the Holy Couple offering it together. A humble admission of lowliness, concern for the poor and oppressed, a yearning for justice, great joy at the coming of God's kingdom—the themes of the prayer fit them both. Perhaps Mary and Joseph used its phrases as they thanked God together for their marriage and family life and what he would accomplish through it: "The Mighty One has done great things for us! Holy is his name!" (see Luke 1:49).

At Cana, Always. Every couple who enters into the sacrament of marriage can count on the grace of God's continuing presence. "Just as of old God encountered his people with a covenant of love and fidelity, so our Savior, the Spouse of the Church, now encounters Christian spouses through the sacrament of marriage. He abides with them." (*The Church in the Modern World*, section 48). As Father Jacques Leclercq puts it, "God becomes as it were a third party in the intimacy of married life."

You might say that Jesus' mother and earthly father become party to our marriages as well.

The mother of Christ is the mother of the body of Christ, the Church. Given to us in a special way at Calvary (John 19:26–27), she watches over us with the same sensitive concern and effective intercession she showed a couple who ran out of wine at their wedding celebration (John 2:1–10).

As for Joseph, by virtue of his marriage to Mary, he is "patron of the universal Church." John Paul II observes: "The Church is in fact the Body of Christ. Wasn't it therefore logical and necessary that the one to whom the eternal Father confided his Son would also extend his protection over the Church?"

Like parents who keep loving and helping children who have left the family nest, the Holy Couple still watches over Christ's body by caring for us. They, too, are present in the "Cana forever" journey of every Christian marriage.

Suggestions for Bible Discussion Groups

L ike a camping trip, a Bible discussion group works best if you agree on where you're going and how you intend to get there. Many groups use their first meeting to talk over such questions. Here is a checklist of issues, with bits of advice from people who have experience in Bible discussions. (A planning discussion will go more smoothly if the leaders have thought through the following issues beforehand.)

Agree on your purpose. Are you getting together to gain wisdom and direction for your lives? to finally get acquainted with the Bible? to support one another in following Christ? to encourage those who are exploring—or reexploring—the Church? for other reasons?

Agree on attitudes. For example: "We're all beginners here." "We're here to help one another understand and respond to God's word." "We're not here to offer counseling or direction to one another." "We want to read Scripture prayerfully." What do *you* wish to emphasize? Make it explicit!

Agree on ground rules. Barbara J. Fleischer, in her useful book *Facilitating for Growth,* recommends that a group clearly state its approach to the following:

- *Preparation.* Do we agree to read the material and prepare answers to the questions before each meeting?
- *Attendance.* What kind of priority will we give to our meetings?
- *Self-revelation.* Are we willing to help the others in the group gradually get to know us—our weaknesses as well as our strengths, our needs as well as our gifts?
- *Listening.* Will we commit ourselves to listen to one another?
- *Confidentiality.* Will we keep everything that is shared *with* the group *in* the group?
- *Discretion.* Will we refrain from sharing about the faults and sins of people who are not in the group?
- *Encouragement and support.* Will we give as well as receive?
- *Participation.* Will we give each person the time and opportunity to make a contribution?

You could probably take a pen and draw a circle around *listening* and *confidentiality.* Those two points are especially important.

The following items could be added to Fleischer's list:

♦ *Relationship with parish.* Is our group part of the adult faith-formation program? independent but operating with the express approval of the pastor? not a parish-based group?

♦ *New members.* Will we let new members join us once we have begun the six weeks of discussions?

Agree on housekeeping.

♦ *When will we meet?*

♦ *How often will we meet?* Meeting weekly or every other week is best if you can manage it. William Riley remarks, "Meetings once a month are too distant from each other for the threads of the last session not to be lost" (*The Bible Study Group: An Owner's Manual*).

♦ *How long will each meeting run?*

♦ *Where will we meet?*

♦ *Is any setup needed?* Christine Dodd writes that "the problem with meeting in a place like a church hall is that it can be very soul-destroying," given the cold, impersonal feel of many church facilities. If you have to meet in a church facility, Dodd recommends doing something to make the area homey (*Making Scripture Work*).

♦ *Who will host the meetings?* Leaders and hosts are not necessarily the same people.

♦ *Will we have refreshments?* Who will provide them? Don Cousins and Judson Poling make this recommendation: "Serve refreshments if you like, but save snacks and other foods for the end of the meeting to minimize distractions"(*Leader's Guide 1*).

♦ *What about child care?* Most experienced leaders of Bible discussion groups discourage bringing infants or other children to adult Bible discussions.

Agree on leadership. You need someone to facilitate—to keep the discussion on track, to see that everyone has a chance to speak, to help the group stay on schedule. Rena Duff, editor of the newsletter *Sharing God's Word Today,* recommends having two or three people take turns leading the discussions.

It's okay if the leader is not an expert on the Bible. You have this Six Weeks book as a guide, and if questions come up that no one can answer, you can delegate a participant to do a little research between meetings. Perhaps your parish priest or someone on the pastoral staff of your parish could offer advice. Or help may be available from your diocesan catechetical office or a local Catholic college or seminary.

It's important for the leader to set an example of listening, to draw out the quieter members (and occasionally restrain the more vocal ones), to move the group on when it gets stuck, to get the group back on track when the discussion moves away from the topic, and to restate and summarize what the group is learning. Sometimes the leader needs to remind the members of their agreements. An effective group leader is enthusiastic about the topic and the discussions and sets an example of learning from others and of using resources for growing in understanding.

As a discussion group matures, other members of the group will increasingly share in doing all these things on their own initiative.

Bible discussion is an opportunity to experience the fulfillment of Jesus' promise "Where two or three are gathered in my name, I am there among them" (Matthew 18:20). Put your discussion group in Jesus' hands. Pray for the guidance of the Spirit. And have a great time exploring God's word together!

Suggestions for Individuals

Y ou can use this book just as well for individual study as for group discussion. While discussing the Bible with other people can be a rich experience, there are advantages to reading on your own. For example:

♦ You can focus on the points that interest you most.
♦ You can go at your own pace.
♦ You can be completely relaxed and unashamedly honest in your answers to all the questions, since you don't have to share them with anyone!

   Our suggestions for using this book on your own are these:

♦ Don't skip "Questions to Begin" or "First Impression."
♦ Take your time on "Questions for Reflection and Discussion." While a group will probably not have enough time to work on all the questions, you can allow yourself the time to consider all of them if you are using the book by yourself.
♦ After reading "Exploring the Theme," go back and reread the Scripture text before answering the Questions for Reflection and Discussion.
♦ Take the time to look up all the parenthetical Scripture references.
♦ Read additional sections of Scripture related to the excerpts in this book. For example, read the portions of Scripture that come before and after the sections that form the readings in this Six Weeks book. You will understand the readings better by viewing them in context in the Bible.
♦ Since you control the pace, give yourself plenty of opportunities to reflect on the meaning of the Scripture passages for you. Let your reading be an opportunity for these words to become God's words to you.

Bibles

The following editions of the Bible contain the full set of biblical books recognized by the Catholic Church, along with a great deal of useful explanatory material:

- The Catholic Study Bible (Oxford University Press), which uses the text of the New American Bible
- The Catholic Bible: Personal Study Edition (Oxford University Press), which also uses the text of the New American Bible
- The New Jerusalem Bible, the regular (not the reader's) edition (Doubleday)

Books, Web Sites, and Other Resources

- Karol Wojtyla, *Love and Responsibility,* trans. H. T. Willetts (San Francisco: Ignatius Press, 1993).
- Pope John Paul II, *The Role of the Christian Family in the Modern World* (Boston: Pauline Books & Media, 1981).
- John Paul II, *Letter to Families from Pope John Paul II: 1994 Year of the Family* (Boston: Pauline Books & Media, 1994).
- Josef Pieper, "On Love," in *Faith, Hope, Love,* trans. Richard and Clara Winston (San Francisco: Ignatius Press, 1997).
- C. S. Lewis, *The Four Loves* (New York: Harcourt, Brace & World, 1960).
- St. John Chrysostom, *On Marriage and Family Life,* trans. Catherine P. Roth and David Anderson (Crestwood, NY: St. Vladimir's Seminary Press, 1986).
- *Catechism of the Catholic Church,* second edition (Washington, DC: United States Catholic Conference, 1997), sections 1602–66; 2360–2400.
- Joseph M. Champlin, *Together for Life: A Preparation for Marriage and for the Ceremony* (Notre Dame, IN: Ave Maria Press, 2002).